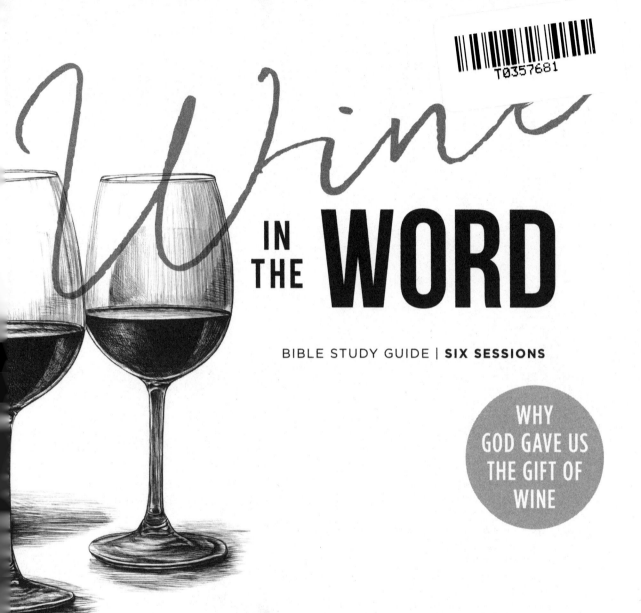

Wine
IN THE WORD

BIBLE STUDY GUIDE | **SIX SESSIONS**

WHY GOD GAVE US THE GIFT OF WINE

GISELA H. KREGLINGER AND RANDY FRAZEE

WITH J.R. BRIGGS

HarperChristian
Resources

Wine in the Word Bible Study Guide
© 2025 by Gisela H. Kreglinger and Randy Frazee

Published in Grand Rapids, Michigan, by HarperChristian Resources. HarperChristian Resources is a registered trademark of HarperCollins Christian Publishing, Inc.

Requests for information should be sent to customercare@harpercollins.com

ISBN 978-0-310-17276-5 (softcover)
ISBN 978-0-310-17277-2 (ebook)

All Scripture quotations are taken from the Holy Bible, New International Version®, NIV®. Copyright © 1973, 1978, 1984, 2011 by Biblica, Inc.® Used by permission. All rights reserved worldwide.

Scripture quotations marked ESV are taken from The Holy Bible, English Standard Version. ESV® Text Edition: 2016. Copyright © 2001 by Crossway Bibles, a publishing ministry of Good News Publishers.

Any internet addresses (websites, blogs, etc.) and telephone numbers in this study guide are offered as a resource. They are not intended in any way to be or imply an endorsement by HarperChristian Resources, nor does HarperChristian Resources vouch for the content of these sites and numbers for the life of this study guide.

HarperChristian Resources titles may be purchased in bulk for church, business, fundraising, or ministry use. For information, please e-mail ResourceSpecialist@ChurchSource.com.

First Printing January 2025 / Printed in the United States of America

Contents

A NOTE FROM GISELA AND RANDY

Greetings!

We want to take you on a journey to discover one of the most amazing gifts that God has given us: the gift of wine. It is the most talked about food in the Bible. There are nearly 1,000 references to wine and wine-related themes stretching from Genesis to Revelation. And yet the church in North America has neglected this important biblical theme and precious, tangible gift. Our difficult history with alcohol, especially distilled spirits, led to the prohibition, and its effects can still be felt today. Wine, like other gifts from God, can be abused. Although we will talk about warnings and boundaries because the Bible does, we will concentrate on the beauty of wine and explore how the Bible presents this gift for our flourishing.

The gift of wine invites us into an embodied, communal, and joyous faith with Christ at the center. You can enter this journey from wherever you are. We know the world of wine can be a bit intimidating, but it should not be that way. As you will learn in session 5, your two presenters have had vastly different introductions to wine, and yet we both have come to appreciate wine with joy, freedom, and a deep sense of gratitude. We will take you on a journey from intimidation to appreciation.

Wine is meant to be shared, so we encourage you to invite others to join you in this exploration, for as we will remind you at times, "the clinking of wine glasses is the sound of togetherness."

With holy cheers,

Gisela and Randy

God gave wine to bless us,
to bring us joy, and to help us
draw near to him.[1]

HOW TO USE THIS GUIDE

Wine and the Bible—it's likely not something you've studied before. In fact, it may be a striking combination to you. Do these two really mix? On the surface, they may seem to be strange bedfellows, but our hope is that through this study you will see just how much overlap exists between the two. This is why we believe the topic is so important.

Our goal in this study is not simply for you to know more *information* about wine in the Bible. Rather, we want you to see all the ways that wine was used in community—in both the Old and New Testaments (including by Jesus)—as people fellowshipped and shared meals together around the table.[2] For this reason, we have developed this study to be as creative, interactive, and *participatory* as possible, so that you can experience this study to the fullest.

With this in mind, we encourage you to engage with others as you go through this content, whether that is a small group, book-discussion group, or any other type of group. (In fact, in the final session of this study, you will be encouraged to experience a wine-tasting exercise together.) As you embark on this journey, know that the videos for each session are available for you to view at any time by following the instructions provided within this study guide.

GROUP STUDY

Each session in this study is divided into two parts: (1) a group-study section, and (2) a personal-study section. The group-study section provides a basic framework on how to open your time together, get the most out of the video content, and discuss the key ideas that were presented. Each session includes the following:

- **Welcome:** A short opening note about the topic of the session for you to read on your own before you meet as a group.
- **Connect:** A few icebreaker questions to get you and your group members thinking about the topic and interacting with each other.
- **Watch:** An outline of the key points covered in each video teaching along with space for you to take notes as you watch each session. (If your group is

comfortable with having a glass of wine while you are watching the video and then discussing, please have that arranged before starting.)

- **Discuss:** Questions to help you and your group reflect on the teaching material presented and apply it to your lives.
- **Respond:** A short personal exercise to help reinforce the key ideas.
- **Practice:** A place for you to record prayer requests and praises for the week.

Make sure you have your own copy of the study guide so you can write down your thoughts, responses, and reflections in the space provided—and so you have access to the videos via streaming. You will also want to have a copy of *Cup Overflowing*, as reading the book alongside this guide will provide you with deeper insights. (See the notes at the beginning of each group session and personal-study section on which chapters of the book you should read before the next group session.)

Finally, keep these points in mind:

- **Facilitation:** If you are doing this study in a group, you will want to appoint someone to serve as a facilitator. This person will be responsible for starting the video and keeping track of time during discussions and activities. If *you* have been chosen for this role, there are some resources in the back of this guide that can help you lead your group through the study.

- **Faithfulness:** Your group is a place where tremendous growth can happen as you reflect on the Bible, ask questions, and learn what God is doing in other people's lives. For this reason, be fully committed and attend each session so you can build trust and rapport with the other members.

- **Friendship:** The goal of any small group is to serve as a place where people can share, learn about God, and build friendships. So seek to make your group a "safe place." Be honest about your thoughts and feelings, but also listen carefully to everyone else's thoughts, feelings, and opinions. Keep anything personal that your group members share in confidence so that you can create a community where people can heal, be challenged, and grow spiritually.

As already mentioned, *Wine in the Word* is intended for use in a group. However, if you are going through this study on your own, read the opening Welcome section and reflect on the questions in the Connect section. Watch the video and use the outline provided to help you take notes. Finally, personalize the questions and exercises in the Discuss and Respond sections. Adapt it to your life so it will be as personal and engaging as possible. Close by recording any requests you want to pray about during the week.

PERSONAL STUDY

The personal study is for you to work through on your own during the week. Each exercise is designed to help you explore the key ideas you uncovered during your group time and delve into passages of Scripture that will help you apply those principles to your life. Go at your own pace, doing a little each day—or you can tackle the material all at once. Remember to spend a few moments in silence to listen to whatever the Holy Spirit might be saying to you.

Each section contains three personal studies that open with a devotion for you to read, several passages to look up, and reflection questions to help you apply what you are learning to your own life. Following this, there is a Connect and Discuss page with several questions for you to answer with a friend, either over a phone call, on a walk, over a cup of coffee, or—better yet—over a good glass of wine! Finally, the Catch Up and Read Ahead page will allow you to finish any uncompleted personal studies and read the upcoming chapters in the book.

If you are doing this study as part of a group and are unable to finish the personal studies for the week, still attend the group time. Be assured you are wanted and welcome, even if you don't have your prep work completed. The group and personal studies are intended to help you delve deeper into the content and apply it to your own life. As you go through this study, listen for where God may want to encourage, teach, remind, guide, or challenge you. We hope this is not only an enlightening and fulfilling study but one where you have meaningful interactions and are able to "taste and see that the Lord is good" (Psalm 34:8) in the most tangible way possible!

WEEK 1

BEFORE GROUP MEETING	Read chapters 2–4 in *Cup Overflowing* Read the Welcome section (page 2)
GROUP MEETING	Discuss the Connect questions Pour a glass of wine and watch the video for session 1 Discuss the questions that follow as a group Do the closing exercise and pray (pages 2–6)
STUDY 1	Complete the personal study (pages 9–12)
STUDY 2	Complete the personal study (pages 13–15)
STUDY 3	Complete the personal study (pages 16–19)
CONNECT AND DISCUSS	Get together and watch the film *The Taste of Things* Discuss the follow-up questions (page 20)
CATCH UP AND READ AHEAD (BEFORE WEEK 2 GROUP MEETING)	Read chapters 1 and 5 in *Cup Overflowing* Complete any unfinished personal studies (page 21)

SESSION *One*

MAKING HUMAN HEARTS GLAD
Why God Gave Us the Gift of Wine

He makes grass grow for the cattle,
And plants for people to cultivate—
Bringing forth food from the earth:
wine that gladdens human hearts,
oil to make their faces shine,
and bread that sustains their hearts.

PSALM 104:14–15

WELCOME | READ ON YOUR OWN

Wine is a great mystery and a profound gift. In the ancient world, it was consumed frequently. It carried medicinal and healing benefits. It was a valuable trade commodity. In biblical times, it was both a tangible gift from God and a sign of his blessing, eliciting joy and suggesting abundance. Yet we don't read much about what Jesus ate and drank. So it may be a bit striking—even discomforting—for us to realize that he not only enjoyed good food at dinner parties but also good *wine*. In fact, Jesus was once accused by his fellow Jews of being "a glutton and a drunkard" (Luke 7:34).

Today, many of us hold strong convictions about wine and alcohol and, for this reason, feel deep emotions around the topic. Maybe you grew up in a church where alcohol was forbidden. Or maybe you were raised in a home where abuse and addiction left scars on a family member or friend. Or maybe you worship in a denominational tradition where alcohol was not only acceptable but also encouraged, celebrated, and consumed with wisdom, joy, and delight. Wherever you have come from, or whatever your context may be, it is important to consider your own personal experience as a starting point to this study.

As you will learn in this study, wine is a significant theme in the Bible. It's the most talked about food in Scripture, yet we pay little attention to it in the church.[3] Furthermore, Jesus lived in a region of the world where wine was produced *abundantly*—long before he was born— and once again is produced there today. Jesus grew up around it, partook in it, told stories about it, and famously transformed water into wine. This study will help you see how you can engage with wine wisely, see it as a God-given gift, and learn to savor and relish it as you experience firsthand the joy and blessing of what God has given to you.

CONNECT | 15 MINUTES

If you or any of your group members don't know each other, take a few minutes to introduce yourselves. Then discuss one or both of the following questions:

- What was it that drew you to this particular study? What are you hoping to glean from the next handful of weeks together?

— *or* —

- As you think about your own experience, what are your thoughts, feelings, and convictions around wine and alcohol, more widely speaking?

WATCH | 20 MINUTES

If your group is comfortable with having a glass of wine while watching the video, have that arranged before you begin. Note that the video can be accessed by playing the DVD or through streaming (see the instructions provided with this guide). Below is an outline of the key points covered in the teaching. Record any key concepts that stand out to you.

OUTLINE

I. The Bible contains nearly 1,000 references to wine and wine-related themes.
   A. We are to cultivate a sense of awe and wonder for God, marveling at all he has made.
   B. God is the one who provides, not just for humans but for all of creation.
   C. We are to enjoy wine as part of God's creation that he has entrusted to our care.

II. The Bible tells us that wine gladdens the heart (Psalm 104:14–15).
   A. Wine connects and embeds us into the wider community of God's creation.
   B. Wine brings us around the table, where human community is at its best.
   C. When consumed appropriately and wisely, wine helps us to relax, savor, and enjoy.

III. God calls us to use all our senses when it comes to engaging in our faith.
   A. A question worth asking: *Are our taste buds attuned to the good news in liquid form?*
   B. When we think of our faith, we tend to draw on our mind and emotions and senses, such as hearing (listening to a sermon) and seeing (reading the Bible).
   C. We need to relearn how to draw on *all* our senses in our pursuit of knowing God.

IV. The first mention of wine in the Bible is when Noah planted a vineyard (Genesis 9:20).
   A. This was an act of faith for Noah, as it takes four to five years before a vineyard bears fruit.
   B. We immediately read that Noah got drunk after planting the vineyard (see Genesis 9:21).
   C. Noah was not judged for this; instead, his youngest son, Ham, and his son, Canaan, were judged for not protecting their father's honor and reputation.

V. We must engage with wine wisely and with discernment.
   A. God has given wine as a gift, but we have to be careful not to abuse it.
   B. Proverbs offers many examples of how to approach wine (see, for example, 3:9–10; 9:5–6; 20:1–3; 31:6).
   C. Drinking in moderation connects us to God's creation and draws us together in fellowship.

NOTES

_____
_____
_____
_____
_____
_____
_____
_____
_____
_____
_____
_____
_____
_____
_____
_____
_____
_____
_____
_____

DISCUSS | 35 MINUTES

Discuss what you just watched by answering the following questions.

1. The fact there are nearly 1,000 references to wine and wine-related themes in the Bible reveals that wine is a big deal in the Bible and, consequently, a big deal to God and what he wants to communicate to us through it. What were your experiences with wine growing up in your home? What are your experiences with wine in the church?

2. Have someone in the group read Psalm 104:14–15 aloud—slowly and twice. Reflect on the phrase "wine that gladdens human hearts." When you hear that statement, is it more encouraging or unsettling for you? Explain your response.

3. Psalm 104 helps us to not only see that we depend on God's generous blessing in our lives but also that wine (as well as oil and bread) can bring out the blessing and deep joy found in human community. Have you seen these play out in your life or in the lives of others? If so, tell a brief story about when you've experienced that.

4. Ask someone to read aloud Genesis 27:25–29. This passage is a blessing that Isaac bestowed on his son Jacob. What does Isaac say about wine as part of that blessing? Why do you think Isaac might have included that statement in his words to Jacob?

5. Have a different person in the group read Proverbs 23:19–22. John Chrysostom, an early church father, penned these words: "Wine was given to make us cheerful, not to make us behave shamefully; to make us laugh, not a laughing-stock; to make us healthy, not sick; to mend the weakness of the body, not to undermine the soul."[4] One of the goals of this study is to help you see that wine, when used appropriately, can be a gift from God. What does this passage say about the importance of wisdom when it comes to engaging with wine in ways that are pleasing to the Lord? What does it mean for you to appropriately and wisely engage with wine in your life?

RESPOND | 5 MINUTES

King Solomon, who received the gift of incredible wisdom from God, wrote, "Go, eat your food with gladness, and drink your wine with a joyful heart" (Ecclesiastes 9:7). Wine *is* a gift from God but, like many other good things in life, it needs to be consumed wisely and in moderation. Life is fraught with tensions and temptations, but it is in those places that Christ wants to meet us with love and grace, healing our ways of consumption, including our patterns of consuming food, wine, and alcohol more widely speaking.[5]

How has your family of origin and/or faith tradition informed and shaped how you have viewed wine in the past? How has it shaped how you view it today?

Has your thinking about wine and alcohol changed over time at all? If so, how—and what have been the factors that have informed that change?

PRAY | 10 MINUTES

Praying for each other is one of the most important ways you engage in community. In group settings, it can be tempting to see a closing time of prayer as an obligatory way to end your time together. Instead, use this important time as a way to support, challenge, and encourage one another in specific ways, while also stretching your own faith and opening yourselves more fully to God's healing presence. Before you begin praying, go around the group and have each person answer this question: What is it specifically that I long for God to do in me in this study? After everyone finishes sharing, pray for what was said and ask God to answer those requests.

Personal Study

As you heard this week, the Bible has much to teach us about wine. In particular, God has given us wine to bless his people and, thus, it can help us appreciate the bountiful generosity of our God who loves us unconditionally. This week, you will explore a few more passages not only on the subject of wine but also on your senses—and how God has created them to help you experience him through the beautiful world that he has made. Before you begin, prepare yourself by asking God to show exactly what you need and what he desires for you to know. As you work through the questions, write down your thoughts, questions, concerns, insights, and prayers. If you are reading *Cup Overflowing* alongside this study, you may want to first review chapters 2–4.

It is time to reclaim the gift of wine;
the gift of our senses of touch, taste, and
smell in our pursuit of knowing God.[6]

EXPERIENCING GOD WITH ALL OUR SENSES

As mentioned in the group time, we tend to press into faith most often with our mind and our emotions, drawing on our senses of hearing and seeing. However, God has created us with more senses through which we experience the world: touch, smell, and taste. What if these senses could also usher us into a deeper connection with our benevolent God? What if God created this world so we could commune with him through his good creation and the bountiful food, including wine, it brings forth (see Genesis 1:29; 2:8–9, Psalm 104:13–15)?

When COVID-19 first impacted the world in 2020, many people who contracted the virus lost their senses of smell and taste. These individuals grieved the absence of enjoying tasty food and pleasurable aromas. Fortunately, most of these people have regained these senses and report finding newfound appreciation and deepened gratitude for the ability to taste things again like fish tacos or smell the fragrant aromas of fresh-ground coffee (not to mention the distinct tastes and fragrances of a glass of wine).

Take a moment to think about your five senses.

What is the best *taste* you've ever experienced?

What are the most beautiful *sounds* you've ever heard?

What are most awe-inspiring things you've ever *seen*—those things that struck you with awe and wonder?

What are the *smells* that bring a smile to your face and retrieve fond memories?

What is the softest thing you've *touched*, and what did that evoke in you?

God made the world to be beautiful. He gave you the sensitivity and ability to notice beauty. And God has made you not merely to receive these things for survival—like air, water and food—but also to enjoy them intensely and, through their enjoyment, commune with the Giver of all gifts . . . including delicious food and fragrant wine!

READ | Leviticus 23:9–13; Numbers 18:25–27; Deuteronomy 14:22–23, 15:12–15

REFLECT

1. Take a reading on how you're engaging with the topic of this study so far. On a scale of 1 to 10 (with 1 being low and 10 being high), how would you assess what you are thinking, feeling, and sensing?

Your level of concern discussing wine in the Bible:

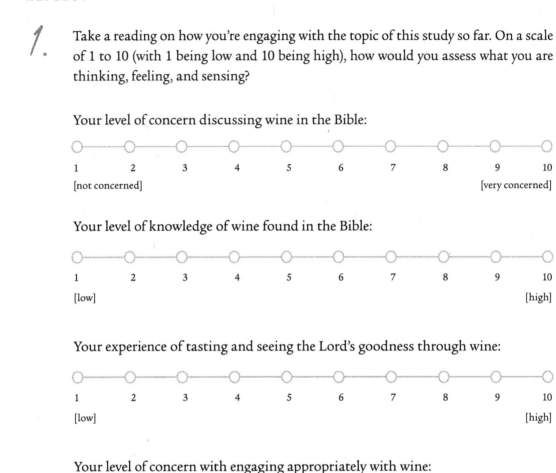

| 1 | 2 | 3 | 4 | 5 | 6 | 7 | 8 | 9 | 10 |
[not concerned]   [very concerned]

Your level of knowledge of wine found in the Bible:

| 1 | 2 | 3 | 4 | 5 | 6 | 7 | 8 | 9 | 10 |
[low]   [high]

Your experience of tasting and seeing the Lord's goodness through wine:

| 1 | 2 | 3 | 4 | 5 | 6 | 7 | 8 | 9 | 10 |
[low]   [high]

Your level of concern with engaging appropriately with wine:

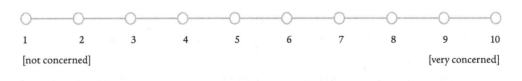

| 1 | 2 | 3 | 4 | 5 | 6 | 7 | 8 | 9 | 10 |
[not concerned]   [very concerned]

Your level of concern discussing wine with other Christians:

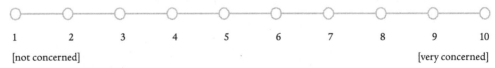

| 1 | 2 | 3 | 4 | 5 | 6 | 7 | 8 | 9 | 10 |
[not concerned]   [very concerned]

2. As you read the passages about God commanding his people to bring offerings to him, which included wine, what did you notice? What are some of the repeated themes that emerge? Does anything surprise you about the fact that God would *command* this as an offering from his people? What was its purpose?

3. When was the last time you tasted and saw the goodness of the Lord (such as experiencing an amazing meal with friends or witnessing the glory of a beautiful hydrangea in full bloom)? What did that reveal—or what might that reveal—about God's goodness?

The Jewish and Christian faiths uphold that our bodies, including the five senses, are a gift from God—a gift to be embraced, treasured, and celebrated. And yet in the Western Christian tradition, there is often a lingering suspicion toward the senses of touch, smell, and taste, and how they might aid us in our pursuit of sensing God's presence among us. We need to rediscover and affirm our God-given senses as the only way through which we can come to know and sense God's presence with us. A glass of wine can help us rediscover our senses of touch, taste, and smell as we learn to notice subtle tastes and intricate aromas and feel new sensations in our mouths and bodies. Wine can not only help reawaken forgotten senses but also invites us to linger in the present moment. Wine can instill a sense of awe and wonder in us for the beautiful world that God has made and that we get to experience through all our senses. What a gift![7]

4. Do this short exercise. Find something that engages one of your senses (holding a soft blanket, listening to a favorite song, smelling and tasting a small piece of dark chocolate, savoring a sip of wine). Take a few moments to truly experience it, relish it, and savor it. What is it that you appreciate or experience through your senses?

5. What might be some factors keeping you from experiencing God's goodness through each of your senses? How can you avoid dualistic thinking (earthly joys should be avoided while only heavenly things can be good) when it comes to God and his creation?

PRAY | End your personal study time by writing a prayer of gratitude and praise to God for creating your senses in ways that allow you to experience his goodness through the world he created. Be as specific and personal as you can in expressing that gratitude to him.

FAITH-FILLED PLANTING FOR THE FUTURE

When you think of wine, you might picture the sprawling vineyards of Napa Valley or some of the great vineyards in Europe. However, wine making is not a new phenomenon. Wine has been around for thousands of years and is made in places all across the earth—including the Holy Land. In fact, the most ancient wine cellar that archaeologists have found is near the mountain range of Ararat, where Noah's ark came to rest after the flood. Scholars suggest the wine cellar might be more than 6,000 years old—which is probably long before Noah arrived on the scene.

When you read the story of Noah in the Bible, your mind almost certainly goes to the account of how God, seeing all the wickedness that was on the earth, determined to wipe out humanity by sending a great flood. Only Noah and his family were found to be righteous, so the Lord instructed them to build a wooden ark and take into it two of every "unclean" animal (male and female) and seven pairs of "clean" animals. After this, God sent the flood, sparing Noah, his family, and all the living creatures who were taken into the ark.

Yet Noah's story doesn't end there! As you learned in the group time this week, Noah became a vintner after the waters of the flood receded on the earth. He tended the soil and planted a vineyard. In fact, it is the first thing the Bible records that Noah did after the Lord made a covenant with him and promised to never send another flood on the earth.

It takes a relatively long time (four to five years) before a vineyard produces a significant harvest of grapes. This means that Noah's act of planting the vineyard required immense hope on his part and a deep faith that God would provide a better future. It required a deep trust and belief in God's future work. This has profound theological implications for our lives even today.

READ | Genesis 9:18–29

REFLECT

1. Reread the portion of this passage below. Underline any word, detail, or phrase you find surprising. Put a question mark next to anything that seems perplexing.

> Noah, a man of the soil, proceeded to plant a vineyard. When he drank some of its wine, he became drunk and lay uncovered inside his tent. Ham, the father of Canaan, saw his father naked and told his two brothers outside. But Shem and Japheth took a garment and laid it across their shoulders; then they walked in backward and covered their father's naked body. Their faces were turned the other way so that they would not see their father naked. When Noah awoke from his wine and found out what his youngest son had done to him, he said, "Cursed be Canaan! The lowest of slaves will he be to his brothers." He also said, "Praise be to the LORD, the God of Shem! May Canaan be the slave of Shem. May God extend Japheth's territory; may Japheth live in the tents of Shem, and may Canaan be the slave of Japheth."

2. Look back on what you underlined or questioned. What is the *most* surprising thing that you found in this passage? What is the *most* perplexing to you?

3. Think about Noah's planting the vineyard as an act of faith. What are some acts of faith you and your community (family, church, and the like) have made in the past that were not decisions made for that particular moment but for the future—ones that required deep trust in God for your future? What have you witnessed in your life and your community as a result of making those acts of faith?

4. Reflect on a few of these kinds of "vineyard planting" acts of faith you could make that would require a deep trust in God for the wellbeing of your future. These could be planting a fruit-bearing tree in your neighborhood, helping with a local community garden, preparing a meal for a feast, or initiating or investing in relationships. Write these below, and then consider with whom might it be wise to share your ideas.

5. We do not find God judging Noah for getting drunk. However, we do see Noah judging Ham (and Ham's son Canaan) for what he did. Ham, instead of protecting his father's honor, damaged it by gossiping about what happened. Although drunkenness is spoken against in the Bible (in Proverbs and other places), why do you think Noah was not judged here? Why do you think Ham (and his family) was judged so severely by Noah for his actions?

PRAY | End your time by thanking God for his continued faithfulness. Ask that he would give you the same posture of faith for your community's future that Noah had for his family and descendants as you trust his goodness and faithfulness. Write out a few lines below to pray honestly, personally, and boldly to God.

ENGAGING WITH GOD'S GIFT WISELY

Knowledge is good, but wisdom is better. We live in a world that doesn't cherish wisdom; in fact, there are many ways our culture instead praises and values immediate gratification, overindulgence, and shortsightedness. So one of the most important ways we can honor the Lord is by living a life in intentional pursuit of godly wisdom.

The Bible provides a lot of wisdom on how God wants us to live—including how we should wisely engage with and consume God's good gift of wine. The book of Proverbs especially is filled with this kind of insight. This wisdom from the Lord is not a passing fad that works for a short season; it has stood the test of time and applies to our lives to this day.

It is important to point out that you can't obtain this kind of godly wisdom automatically. Nobody "drifts" into wisdom. Rather, you receive it when you value it highly and proactively pursue it together as God's people. Wisdom will grow in you and your community when you "choose [God's] instruction instead of silver" and his "knowledge rather than choice gold," knowing that "wisdom is more precious than rubies, and nothing you desire can compare with her" (Proverbs 8:10–11).

Think about this statement from Proverbs. At the time this passage was written, silver, gold, and rubies were among the finest and most valuable materials a person could possess—just as they are highly coveted and prized in the world today. Even so, the author of this proverb could state, based on his experience, that godly wisdom was to be even more highly valued. This should cause each of us to pause and ask: *Do we actually believe that wisdom has this kind of value in our lives and in the lives of those who are close to us?*

This is what you will explore today.

READ | Proverbs 3:9–10; 9:1–6; 20:1; 23:20–22; 31:4–7

REFLECT

1. In Proverbs 3:9–10, we see how important agricultural offerings/tithings were in helping the Jewish people understand that everything the earth brings forth is a gift from God, including wine. Offerings were a vehicle of prayer, and through them, they grew in their sense of awe and wonder for their holy God and how he provided for them. Through these offerings, the people expressed their gratitude to God for the gifts of food and wine. Today, most of us do not grow food or bring it as an offering to church. In what ways has this removed us from appreciating God's creation? How can you reconnect with creation either by growing some of your food (like herbs or tomatoes) or by supporting a local farmer at a farmer's market?

2. In Proverbs 9:1–6, the invitation to receive and gain wisdom is compared to an industrious and hospitable woman who opens her home and prepares a feast that includes rich food and wine. Think about this female personification of wisdom. Ponder why hospitality, feasting together, and rich food and wine are used to speak about the wisdom God offers to us and desires for us to share, consume, and digest like delicious food and wine. What is it about sharing wine at a feast that could speak to the wisdom God desires to give to us? (Remember that in the Hebrew worldview, wine was seen as a valuable gift and blessing from God. It elevated daily meals, enriched religious celebrations, strengthened a sense of community, and brought joy, pleasure, and comfort amidst the hardships of daily life.)

3. Given that wine was held in such high esteem, it is perhaps not surprising that Proverbs also includes some stern warnings against drunkenness and the abuse of wine. What are these warnings in relation to wine as given in Proverbs 20:1 and 23:20–22? List them below.

Proverbs 23:30–35 describes the sad state of drunkenness and hangover experienced the next morning in quite some detail. Why do you think it is included here? What purpose does this have in the context of the pursuit of wisdom?

In Proverbs 31:4–5, leaders are discouraged from consuming too much wine and alcohol. What dangers are described here? Be specific as you list them.

4. Proverbs 31:6–7 seems to give people permission to consume strong drink and wine when they experience severe suffering, such as at the end of their lives or when they are in severe anguish. What do you make of this passage? Does it surprise you? Explain your response.

In ancient times, wine and alcohol might have had the role that painkillers have today. Given that we live in a culture where people numb themselves with substances (like alcohol, food, and drugs) and activities of various kinds (such as social media scrolling, binge watching, or shopping) on a regular basis, how are we to understand and apply this passage with wisdom?

5. Proverbs ends by celebrating the noble, wise, and industrious wife who exemplifies wisdom in all she does (see 31:10–20). Like Noah, she plants a vineyard (see verse 16). What do you think is the meaning of this, given that wine abuse is a major theme in Proverbs?

How does this passage bring the theme of wine to a close in Proverbs?

Given the description of the wife's character and life, how do you think she handled the drinking of wine in her family?

PRAY | Close your time by considering your own family, community, and church context. Is it possible to have an open and honest conversation about wine and alcohol in your family, with your church community, or with your friends? Ask the Lord to give you wisdom in how to address the subject matter of wine. (Later in this study, you will be encouraged to develop wisdom for how to consume wine wisely.)

CONNECT AND DISCUSS

This study in *Wine in the Word* is not intended to just give you knowledge about the joys of wine but to also encourage you to experience those joys for yourself.

Wine is a gift that is to carry God's blessings into our communities. In the Bible, wine's role is to open our lives to the Giver of all good things, deepen our sense of joy that we are his beloved, and bring ease and comfort to us in the humdrum of our stressful and busy lives. The beauty and complexity of wine hints at a reality much greater than what our eyes can see, our hands can touch, our tongues can taste, and our noses can smell. Wine hints at the unfathomable generosity of our Creator and Redeemer, who invites us into his presence to linger and to be filled with his love and grace and joy.[8]

With this in mind, gather with some friends and/or group members this week and have an informal movie night. The film to watch is a 2023 romantic drama called *The Taste of Things,* which is a French-language film with English subtitle (the run time is 2 hours and 14 minutes). Set on a picturesque country estate in France in 1889, the film depicts the romance between Eugénie (played by Juliette Binoche), a cook, and Dodin (played by Benoît Magimel), a gourmand who delights in her cooking. Ask each person to bring a food item to the movie night—either light snacks like meats, cheeses, olives, fruits, bread, crackers, or more substantial items that you can share together as a meal. Also, as with all of the times that you will meet during the week, have someone bring some lovely wine!

Before you begin the film, have each person briefly share what stuck out to them in this session—a verse, question, insight, connection, reminder, or anything else. Serve the light snacks or the meal with the wine and have everyone focus on their senses of touch, taste, and smell. When the movie concludes, take a few minutes to discuss the following.

- Is there anything you studied this week that connects with what you saw in the film? If so, which things connect?

- How might the engagement of your senses, which God has graciously given to you to enjoy him and his world, help you appreciate more of who God is?

- How have you experienced joy, pleasure, or delight this week through your senses? How could you thank God for giving you the ability to experience this joy?

- How has this week's study encouraged you to seek out wisdom more earnestly?

CATCH UP AND READ AHEAD

Use this time to complete any study and reflection questions that you were unable to finish over the past week. Make a note below of any questions that still linger. Reflect on any new insights or awareness you've gleaned as well as any areas of growth you are discerning.

Read chapters 1 and 5 in *Cup Overflowing* before the next group session. Use the space below to note anything that stood out to you, encouraged you, or challenged you.

WEEK 2

BEFORE GROUP MEETING	Read chapters 1 and 5 in *Cup Overflowing* Read the Welcome section (page 24)
GROUP MEETING	Discuss the Connect questions Pour a glass of wine and watch the video for session 2 Discuss the questions that follow as a group Do the closing exercise and pray (pages 24–28)
STUDY 1	Complete the personal study (pages 31–33)
STUDY 2	Complete the personal study (pages 34–37)
STUDY 3	Complete the personal study (pages 38–41)
CONNECT AND DISCUSS	Get together for a meal or snacks (with wine) Discuss the follow-up questions (page 42)
CATCH UP AND READ AHEAD (BEFORE WEEK 4 GROUP MEETING)	Read chapters 11–15 in *Cup Overflowing* Complete any unfinished personal studies (page 43)

SESSION *Two*

WATER INTO WINE
The Best Is Yet to Come

*Jesus said to the servants, "Fill the jars with water";
so they filled them to the brim. Then he told them,
"Now draw some out and take it to the master of the banquet."
They did so, and the master of the banquet tasted the water
that had been turned into wine. . . . Then he called the
bridegroom aside and said, "Everyone brings out the choice
wine first and then the cheaper wine after the guests have had
too much to drink; but you have saved the best till now."*

JOHN 2:7–10

WELCOME | READ ON YOUR OWN

Have you ever read something so often or heard a story so frequently that you tune out without realizing it? It could be something your boss says or a story told at a family reunion. Maybe you do it during some of the classic stories found in the Bible.

Perhaps you grew up in a church where you heard those classic stories frequently. Adam and Eve in the garden of Eden. Moses and the parting of the Red Sea. David fighting Goliath. Jonah being swallowed by the big fish. Jesus feeding the five thousand. It can be easy to hear these stories and think, *Yeah, yeah, I've heard this before.*

In this session, we are going to explore one of those classic stories found in the New Testament: Jesus turning water into wine. This is a story that you've undoubtedly heard before—probably many times before. You might be tempted to think, *Yeah, I already know this story.* But as you will discover, there is so much more going on in this story.

First things and last things are important in people's lives and ministries. They announce, mark, and signal to the world what those individuals value and what they want others to remember. In the Gospel of John, we learn that Jesus' first miracle—something meant to mark his ministry—was turning water into wine.[9]

The ancient rabbis believed that Scripture was like a multifaceted gem; if you turn the story just slightly, it shimmers and shines with new scintillating beauty that you hadn't seen before. The challenge for you in this session is to be open to new (and maybe surprising) ways this familiar story will engage your head, heart, and soul. Try to look at this story as if you are reading or hearing it for the first time.

CONNECT | 15 MINUTES

If you or any of your group members don't know each other, take a few minutes to introduce yourselves. Then discuss one or both of the following questions:

- What is something that spoke to your heart or touched one of your senses in last week's personal study that you would like to share with the group?

— *or* —

- What do you know about the story of Jesus turning water into wine at the wedding in Cana? What stands out to you in that story?

WATCH | 20 MINUTES

Once again, if your group is comfortable with having a glass of wine while watching the video, please have that arranged before you begin. Below is an outline of the key points covered in the teaching. Record any key concepts that stand out to you.

OUTLINE

I. The fact that Jesus' first recorded miracle is turning water into wine is significant.
  A. It makes a statement about who Jesus is, where he comes from, and where he wants to take us.
  B. The setting of the miracle is also important: at a wedding feast in the town of Cana.
  C. This is the first of seven "signs," each of which has multiple meanings.

II. Weddings were extremely joyous occasions in the first century (John 2:1–2).
  A. Weddings involved lots of wine, music, and dancing—and lasted up to seven days.
  B. The prolonged joyful celebration served to bond the new family together.
  C. The length of the festivities speaks to the depth of commitment between the parties.

III. Running out of wine was a great embarrassment at the time (John 2:3–5).
  A. It would have put a damper on the celebration and disappointed the guests.
  B. Wine was also seen as a sign of God's blessing on the couple—so you didn't want it to run out!
  C. So Jesus stepped in to change water stored in six nearby stone jars into wine (John 2:6–8).

IV. There is rich meaning in Jesus' miracle of turning the water into wine.
  A. The Old Testament prophets (Amos, Hosea, Joel, Zechariah, Micah, Jeremiah, Isaiah) wrote that an abundance of wine would be a sign of God's future redemption.
  B. This miracle points forward to the heavenly wedding banquet that will occur with the return of Jesus, as the bridegroom, for the church, his bride (Revelation 19:9).

V. Jesus wants to get our attention with this miracle at the wedding feast in Cana.
  A. Jesus didn't make ordinary wine but *choice* wine (John 2:9–10). The salvation that he offers is the *choice* wine that will make the heavenly wedding guests giddy!
  B. A beautiful wine can become a vehicle for prayer and worship—therefore, quality matters.
  C. Wine can and should be a mediator between heaven and earth, the sacred and the secular, and remind us that God is benevolent and generous toward us.

NOTES

_____

_____

_____

_____

_____

_____

_____

_____

_____

_____

_____

_____

_____

_____

_____

_____

_____

DISCUSS | 35 MINUTES

Discuss what you just watched by answering the following questions.

 Ask someone to read John 2:1–11 aloud. As the story is read, imagine yourself as a character in the story—as if you were a guest at the wedding.

- What did you *see* as the story was read? Were there flowers and food on the table? Were there guests mingling and dancing?
- What did you *hear*? Was there talking and laughter? Was there music?
- What did the food *smell* and *taste* like?

2. Weddings were important occasions with lots of wine, music, and dancing. The emphasis was on prolonged celebrations, and the dancing, singing, and feasting bonded the new family together. What do you think it would have been like to celebrate with the newly married couple for *seven days*? What implications would that length of time have socially, relationally, and logistically on the participants?

3. In John 2:1–11, Jesus brings forth a miracle of *extravagant abundance* of wine to intensify and prolong the celebration of ordinary people at the wedding. Jesus is a joyful, active, celebrating participant who likes to provide in abundance for us and who wants to invite more people into celebrations. What does this tell you about Jesus' nature and character? What implications does this have on your community?

4. Jesus not only brought forth a miracle of *abundant* wine but also *exquisite* wine. In your own experience, what makes up a well-structured wine? What is your favorite, and why? What do you think the master of the banquet was seeing, smelling, and tasting when he commented that the wine Jesus had made was "the best" (verse 10)?

5. In the book of Revelation, John writes to the church, "The Spirit and the bride say, 'Come!' And let the one who hears say, 'Come!' Let the one who is thirsty come" (22:17). What is your church thirsty for today? What is it that your church community truly longs to receive from the Lord?

RESPOND | 10 MINUTES

"Feasts and celebrations were an important part of the religious and cultural context in which Jesus grew up. So perhaps it is not surprising that Jesus' first miracle happened at such a festivity."[10] Imagine how different Jesus' miracle would have been if he had turned water into goat's milk, or pomegranate juice, or even more water. All of these are good and necessary things, especially in first-century Israel. But think of the rich meaning that exists because the miracle involved wine, which implies celebration, savoring, and joy. The joy that wine brings comes when God's people gather, celebrate the life that God has given them, and allow the sharing of meals and celebrations of feasts to bring them together in the midst of the challenges and divisions of life.

How can you reach out to someone who is different from you and create a space of joy even in the face of differences and divisions? How can Paul's list of the fruit of the Spirit in Galatians 5:22–23 help you to build bridges and reach out? (Observe how the sharing of wine can help you unite and focus on the common ground you have in Christ.)

The miracle at the wedding in Cana points to the future heavenly wedding banquet that will take place at the marriage supper of the Lamb. Jesus is the bridegroom, and we, the church, are his bride. Read Isaiah 25:6 and Revelation 19:9. What do these verses say about that future celebration? What does it say about our God that he will serve as host at this celebration? How does this inspire you to see feasts and celebrations as ways to cultivate hope and anticipatory joy for what lies ahead in God's future?

PRAY | 10 MINUTES

End your time in a joyful, celebratory posture of prayer. Finish these sentences: (1) *God, we thank you for . . .* (1) *Jesus, we celebrate the fact that you . . .* (3) *Spirit, you are worthy of being celebrated because you . . .* End your time together by saying a hearty and energetic *amen!*

SESSION TWO

Personal Study

This week's personal study will encourage you to tap into your creative side. Some of these exercises may come naturally to you, while others will take you out of your comfort zone. But press into each of them anyway to see where the Lord wants to meet you in these practices. Just as athletes warm up before a competition, take a moment to warm up your heart by whispering this simple prayer: *God, surprise me this week as I do this study.* As in the first week, record your thoughts, feelings, and what you experience through your senses as you work through each study and notice your surroundings. (Perhaps you could read some of it outdoors in a garden or local park.) Feel free to include written prayers or even doodles to connect what you are learning to your life. Be as creative as you desire. If you are reading *Cup Overflowing* alongside this study, first read chapters 1 and 5 in the book. (You may also want to review appendix 2 on the "True Vine" of John 15:1–8.)

The abundance of wine hints at
the abundance of life that God wants
to impart to his followers.[11]

THE FIRST MIRACLE OF JESUS

Think of a wedding you've attended in the past. It could have been for a friend, an extended family member, a coworker, or even your own wedding. Can you remember what you felt during the ceremony? If it was like most traditional wedding ceremonies, it was a fairly somber and serious affair filled with meaningful symbolism—and rightfully so, as the parties are entering into a significant till-death-do-us-part kind of covenant.

Now think about the wedding *reception*. Regardless of how traditional and formal the wedding ceremony might have been, it's a good bet this was not the case with the wedding reception. It was probably quite lively and filled with good food, smiles, music, laughter—and maybe even wine. Again, this is rightfully so, as it is a joyous occasion to celebrate.

Certainly, there are cultural differences that make modern-day weddings much different from those in Israel during the first century. No cake, no deejay, no white wedding dress or tuxedos, and no dance floor (though there was definitely dancing during first-century weddings!). However, what ancient and modern weddings share is a spirit of immense joy and celebration for the couple—a day that will live on in the hearts and minds of all who were present and experienced the commitment made by the couple before God for the rest of their lives.

The story of the miracle at Cana that you explored during your group time this week is rich and multifaceted. In this first personal study you are going to examine the events in more detail. As you do, keep in mind the experiences you've had at wedding receptions.

READ | John 2:1–11 (read in two different translations)

REFLECT

1. Notice the differences in language between the two translations. What details or perspective do you notice that you didn't see during the group study this week? What especially stuck out to you in the wording between the two translations?

2. Remember that first things are important in a person's life and ministry. They signal what a person values and wants others to remember. What is the significance of John recording this event as Jesus' *first* miracle? How does it help you understand the nature and character of Jesus? What does John want you to see as you consider the setting for this miracle?

3. If Jesus had turned water into wine that tasted "just fine," it would still have kept the hosts from being embarrassed. However, Jesus created the *best* wine—and he did so at a point in the festivities that went against the expected cultural order of a wedding. In that day, the hosts served the best wine *first*, when the guests had recently arrived and could appreciate it fully. The lower-quality wine was served *last*, when the guests had already had their fill of the good wine. So, in many ways, Jesus' action could be considered a waste (though generosity is never really a waste). What implications can you draw from the fact that Jesus made the best wine last, even though the guests likely wouldn't have fully appreciated it?

4. Remember the line that Mary, Jesus' mother, said to the servants with the large jars of water: "Do whatever he tells you" (John 2:5). Imagine Mary speaking that same line to you: "Do whatever Jesus tells you." How does that challenge you? In what areas of your life would you be most reluctant to do that—and why? Jesus' miracle brought more joy to the community and saved the host from humiliation and shame. How do you sense that Jesus might want you to embrace more joy in your life and share it with the world?

Jesus wasn't an elitist snob, creating an atmosphere of superiority around his miracle-working wine soiree. On the contrary, he remained in the background, diverting attention away from himself. He loved the people around him and wanted to deepen their sense of joy and convivial celebration. He stepped back so that the gifts of God could touch people's lives and lift their spirits up to their benevolent creator.[12]

5. As you consider this first miracle of Jesus, why do you think he chose to remain in the "background" and not draw attention to himself? As you think about where God calls you to minister, how do you feel about remaining in the "background" even as you minister in Jesus' name?

PRAY | Consider those areas where you sense Jesus wants your attention and is perhaps prompting you to touch someone's else life. Open your hands in a spirit of release and surrender, as well as a posture of receptivity, and silently listen if the Lord has anything to speak to you.

THE VINE AND THE BRANCHES

If we are going to talk about wine throughout this study, then it will be important for us to explore vines and vineyards as well.

Jesus would have been very familiar with vines and vineyards, as would his listeners. He grew up in a time and a culture where cultivating vineyards and crafting wine was one of the major industries in and around Galilee and throughout Jewish culture. It's interesting that the oldest and largest wine cellar belonging to a royal palace was discovered by archaeologists at Tel Kabri, which is about a day's walk from where Jesus grew up in Nazareth. Due to the prevalence of wine and vineyards, it's not difficult to imagine Jesus stomping grapes and celebrating with friends and family as he gave thanks to his Father for a successful grape harvest. The Son of God grew up in a famous and prodigious wine region!

Given this background, today you are going to look at a passage that might be familiar to you—a metaphor that Jesus used of vine and branches. Now, while the passage you will study doesn't specifically relate to wine (it could have included several other vined fruits), one can certainly make the connection to grapes on a vine. It is easy to see Jesus using the metaphor of a vineyard to describe the kind of rich relationship that our heavenly Father wants to have with us personally and communally. Furthermore, of all the plants that serve as a source of food, the grapevine can grow like no other. It can thrive in stony soils and on the steepest hills and is productive in the most adverse agricultural contexts where little else can be grown.[13]

With this caveat and consideration in mind, today you will explore what this important metaphor has to teach about our relationship with Christ.

READ | Psalm 80:8–15; Isaiah 5:1–7; Mark 12:1–9; John 15:1–17

REFLECT

1. In the Old Testament, the vine and the vineyard represented the nation of Israel. In John's Gospel, Jesus speaks of himself as the true vine and compares himself with Israel as the true vine and vineyard. Jesus uses this metaphor to make a bold statement of truth about himself: He (the vine) and those who follow him (the branches) are now God's chosen people. Read the following passages, and then write down what God is saying about his people (the "vine" or "vineyard" in these passages).

Passage	What God is saying about his people (*vine* or *vineyard*)
Psalm 80:8–15	
Isaiah 5:1–7	
Mark 12:1–9	
John 15:1–17	

2. In the parable of the tenants (Mark 12:1–9), the vineyard owner sent servants (prophets) and even his own son (Jesus) to those in his vineyard (the people of Israel), but they rejected him. The reason Jesus was rejected and killed is because he challenged the religious leaders and their hold on power. What parallels do you see in today's world (and perhaps even in your own community)?

Jesus and his followers were intimately familiar with nature and the work of a vinegrower and would have easily understood the many parallels between the world of viticulture and the development and growth of the early Christian community. The threefold image of vinegrower, vine, and branches gives this metaphor its distinctive complexity, reminding one of Paul's image of the body of Christ and its members (see Romans 12:4–5; 1 Corinthians 6:15; 12:12–27). This organic metaphor highlights a profound interdependence, intimate union, and fruitful symbiotic relationship between God the Father, Christ, and his followers, the church.[14]

3. What is different about the John 15:1–17 passage? What different themes emerge?

Take a moment to reflect upon the symbiotic relationship between the vinegrower (God the Father), Jesus (the vine), and the branches (us as the body of Christ). What is the Father's distinct role to play (verses 1–3, 9)?

What is Jesus' distinct role to play (verses 4–5, 9–10, 12–13, 15–17)?

What are the branches' distinct role to play (verses 4–10, 12–14)?

4. Jesus calls his followers repeatedly and urgently to abide in him, and they do so by loving one another (verses 4–17) in a world filled with hatred, violence, and persecution (verses 18–25). Where do you see parallels to our world where hatred, violence, or violent speech has become common?

5. How could feasting together become a way to draw near to Christ and love each other? How can sharing a simple meal together with a glass of wine become a way to enter into the joy of Christ's presence that helps you defy fear, despair, and—yes—even hatred? Could you organize a small feast with the help of your friends to love your community?

PRAY | End your time in twofold prayer. First, spend some time in *confession*, admitting and repenting of the times where you have failed to love those God has placed in your life. Second, spend time in *adoration*, thanking Jesus that he and his teachings are the source of your life and your relationships. Thank the Lord that you don't have to do this alone, for he has provided a community of believers you can depend on and the Holy Spirit to guide, comfort, and empower you (see John 16:7).

Study 3

OLD AND NEW WINESKINS

So far in the personal studies for this week, we've been exploring weddings, vines, and vineyards. Today, we are going to consider how wine is stored.

For us to do this, we first need to dig into the cultural background. In ancient times, wine was not stored in bottles—which means the people of the day missed out on seeing some beautiful wine bottle labels! Rather, wine was stored in large sealed stone vessels or in *wineskins*.

Wineskins were flexible pouches made from animal skins with a spout that made it easy to store, transport, and drink the wine. They were often sealed with a stopper, sometimes made of cork or wood. First used in ancient Greece, these leather pouches were supple, long-lasting, and flexible, which was important for holding wine properly. (Search online for a few images to get a better understanding of what they may have looked like.)

Why was it so important for wineskins to be flexible? The reason is that as the wine fermented, it emitted gases that expanded the container in which it was stored. Wineskins, being made of flexible animal skins, could adapt to the changing movements of the wine. However, this was only true to a point. As a wineskin was used, it lost its elasticity and became brittle. If new wine, which emits gases during fermentation, was poured into an old wineskin that was brittle, the old wineskin would likely crack and burst. This not only ruined the wineskin but also lost all the wine!

The best way to ensure the proper preservation and transportation of a *new* wine was to make sure it was poured into a *new* leather wineskin that was capable of expanding and contracting to the movement of the wine's fermentation process. Today, we will look at how Jesus used this ability to be flexible and stretchable in one of his parables and consider the implications for our lives and communities.

READ | Matthew 9:9–17; Mark 2:15–22; Luke 5:27–38

REFLECT

 1. In the greater context of these passages, Jesus is first seen eating and drinking with sinners (tax collectors) in the home of Matthew (also called Levi), while John the Baptist's disciples and the Pharisees were fasting. When asked why he and his disciples were not fasting, Jesus uses the metaphor of a wedding feast to speak about the advent of God's salvation. He argues that it is unreasonable to ask the wedding guests to fast while the bridegroom is still with them. The times of fasting will surely come again, but right at this moment, the bridegroom is with them—and it is time to feast and rejoice. Who is the bridegroom in this metaphor? Who are the guests? How do you interpret what Jesus is saying here?

2. These verses affirm feasting together as an appropriate and wonderful way to celebrate God's presence with us. The following metaphor that Jesus uses of the old wineskins probably stand for a rigid adherence to religious practices, while the new wineskins stand for the ability to be flexible and discerning, knowing when it is time to feast and when it is time to fast. The very use of the metaphor of wineskins—filled with wine and an important ingredient for feast and celebrations—emphasizes what was so prevalent in Jewish religious life: Feasts were important ways the people lived their faith and celebrated God's deliverance and presence with them. Jesus uses the metaphor of the bridegroom and the wedding feast to speak of God's salvation that has come in him. Sit with this metaphor of Jesus as the bridegroom and us, his followers, as guests of the wedding feast. What does this metaphor tell us about how God views us, the life of salvation, and our relationship with him?

3. It can be tempting to live as if Christ were not present in our midst and miss how God is already at work even though we might not be able to see it. How can you become more attentive, prayerful, and discerning in this regard? Do you need to learn to be more patient as you wait and long for God to act? Explain your response.

4. John's disciples and the Pharisees were fasting—waiting for God to act. Jesus, on the other hand, was already out and about ministering to those who did not deserve it. He brought God's love and grace by accepting the invitation to a lavish feast with the wrong people (see Luke 5:29). This act was a profound gesture of acceptance of sinners and outsiders. Think about your community—your family and your local church body. Is there enough adaptability, flexibility, and openness in that "wineskin" to see Jesus at work in unexpected places and with undeserving sinners?

If not, what are some ways you can change your posture and actions toward those in your community and, perhaps, even more so outside of your community?

5. It seems that both John the Baptist and the Pharisees were firmly set on fasting as a way of anticipating God's promises. Yet Jesus not only feasted but also prepared his followers for the times of fasting that would come again. It takes wisdom, flexibility, and adaptability to know when it is time to feast and when it is time to fast. How rigid is your understanding of fasting and feasting and your community's understanding of these things? Are you given easily to despair about the world and find yourself in a state of mourning? Or do you have a sense that God is here and at work and respond by feasting and celebrating?

Can you see Christ at work in the most unexpected places? If so, in what ways?

PRAY | Pick one of these brief prayer prompts as a way to end your time:

- *Lord, keep me from being an old wineskin as you are producing new wine.*
- *Lord, keep me adaptable to the fermenting movement of your Spirit.*
- *God, forgive me, my family, and my church in any areas where we cling too tightly to old-wineskin thinking, believing, and living.*
- *Jesus, show me where you minister in the most unexpected places and with the most unlikely people—and help me to join with you.*
- *Jesus, give me eyes to see and love those who do not deserve it.*

CONNECT AND DISCUSS

For your time of connection and discussion this week, be intentional about gathering with one or two people for a meal or a time of light snacks and finger food. This could include a charcuterie board of meats, cheeses, olives, fruits, bread, crackers, spreads—and, of course, wine. As you convene and connect during the week, share what you have learned and any insights that stood out to you. Use the questions below to help guide your discussion.

- How have you seen the story of the wedding at Cana differently this past week?

- How are you viewing vines and vineyards in a new way? How might these new insights help to move you more faithfully in the direction of abiding in Christ?

- What did you learn in the exploration of wineskins? In what ways are you becoming more aware of the importance of feasting and fasting and how to integrate them into your life?

- How can the group help and encourage you to see Christ in the most unexpected places and with people you would rather avoid?

CATCH UP AND READ AHEAD

Use this time to complete any study and reflection questions that you were unable to finish over the past week. Make a note below of any questions that still linger. Reflect on any new insights or awareness you've gleaned as well as any areas of growth you are discerning.

Read chapters 11–15 in *Cup Overflowing* before the next group session. Use the space below to make note of anything that stood out to you, encouraged you, or challenged you.

WEEK 3

BEFORE GROUP MEETING	Read chapters 11–15 in *Cup Overflowing* Read the Welcome section (page 46)
GROUP MEETING	Discuss the Connect questions Pour a glass of wine and watch the video for session 3 Discuss the questions that follow as a group Do the closing exercise and pray (pages 46–50)
STUDY 1	Complete the personal study (pages 53–55)
STUDY 2	Complete the personal study (pages 56–60)
STUDY 3	Complete the personal study (pages 61–64)
CONNECT AND DISCUSS	Plan an evening of sharing communion together Discuss the follow-up questions (pages 65–66)
CATCH UP AND READ AHEAD (BEFORE WEEK 4 GROUP MEETING)	Read chapters 6 and 20–23 in *Cup Overflowing* Complete any unfinished personal studies (page 67)

THE LORD'S SUPPER
Wine, Suffering, and Abundance

While they were eating, Jesus took bread, and when he had given thanks, he broke it and gave it to his disciples, saying, "Take and eat; this is my body." Then he took a cup, and when he had given thanks, he gave it to them, saying, "Drink from it, all of you. This is my blood of the covenant, which is poured out for many for the forgiveness of sins. I tell you, I will not drink from this fruit of the vine from now on until that day when I drink it new with you in my Father's kingdom."

MATTHEW 26:26–29

WELCOME | READ ON YOUR OWN

Context is crucial. Have you ever entered a group mid-conversation and said to yourself, "I have no idea what they are talking about"? It can be disorienting, confusing, and sometimes even humorous. We get the sense that if we had some additional information about the conversation, we would be able to understand and therefore engage much more. Sometimes, fortunately, a friend will share the additional information we need, giving us context and background to inform us and including us in the conversation.

Cultural context is important too. For example, in America if someone says, "I'm mad about my flat," we understand the person is upset that her car got a flat tire. But if someone in the United Kingdom says, "I'm mad about my flat," the person could be saying he is really excited about the apartment he just moved into. As the saying goes, *context is king*.

In the same way, we're going to explore something that might be familiar to you: the Lord's Supper (or as some traditions call it, communion or the Eucharist). But to understand the true meaning of it, we need to understand the context from which Jesus was speaking when he shared with his disciples. We also need to understand the rich tradition, history, and story in which the Jewish people were embedded. Without this crucial background and context, we miss out on a lot of texture, richness, and depth. We can, in a sense, feel like we are entering mid-conversation.

In this session, our goal is to provide important background and context to help you understand the Lord's Supper, in all its richness, so you can participate in it with greater meaning. Feel free to pour a glass of wine and settle in for another session together.

CONNECT | 15 MINUTES

Get the session started by choosing one or both of the following questions to discuss:

- What is something that spoke to your heart or touched one of your senses in last week's personal study that you would like to share with the group?

— *or* —

- Think of a meaningful time when you participated in communion. What was it like? What was meaningful or moving about it? With whom did you share it?

WATCH | 20 MINUTES

Pour a glass of wine for everyone who is comfortable in having one and then watch the video for this session. Below is an outline of the key points covered during the teaching. Record any key concepts that stand out to you.

OUTLINE

I. The Lord's Supper is significant and important for followers of Jesus.
   A. This was a special meal that Jesus instituted when he celebrated the Passover meal with his disciples.
   B. Jesus redefined that meal in light of his own life and coming death and resurrection.

II. We must understand the Passover meal in order to understand the Lord's Supper.
   A. The king of Egypt refused to set God's people free from their slavery. So Moses, under the direction of God, unleashed ten plagues on the land (Exodus 7–11).
   B. The final plague involved the death of every firstborn male in the land.
   C. The Israelites were to sacrifice an unblemished lamb and spread its blood over the doorframe of the house. The angel would see the blood and "pass over" the home.
   D. God commanded the Jews to observe the Passover in remembrance (Leviticus 23:4–8). Jesus celebrated it annually with his family and relatives (Matthew 26:17–19, 26–29).

III. The wine used in the Passover meal held great importance for God's people.
   A. In Jesus' time, the Passover celebration included drinking four cups of wine.
   B. The Passover story was reenacted by engaging all senses—a fully embodied experience.
   C. Wine was a sign of God's blessing and signified his promise of deliverance.

IV. Jesus redefined what the symbols in the Passover meal meant for his followers.
   A. Jesus elevated the spiritual meaning of wine to refer to his own blood.
   B. Wine represents the blood of the lamb that was slain for the people's deliverance.
   C. The Lord's Supper represents the climax of the covenant between God and his people.

V. The wine and wine-making process remind us of Jesus' sacrifice for our sins.
   A. Just as grapes must be crushed to craft fine wine, so Jesus needed to die a crushing death to save humanity from sin and set us free.
   B. Wine reminds us of the forgiveness of sins and the healing of our relationships.
   C. In the ancient world, wine was also known for its healing properties. Jesus' blood has the power to cleanse us from sin and heal our wounds.

NOTES

_____
_____
_____
_____
_____
_____
_____
_____
_____
_____
_____
_____
_____
_____
_____
_____
_____
_____
_____

DISCUSS | 35 MINUTES

Discuss what you just watched by answering the following questions.

1. Among Christians, there is a variety of experiences with the Lord's Supper. Some take it yearly or monthly, while others engage with it on a weekly basis. How often does your church community participate in communion? How does your faith community celebrate it—formally, with the elements passed by ushers or given up front; or more informally, perhaps with the elements made available for the congregation to take at any time?

2. For us to understand the Lord's Supper, we first have to understand the Passover. Ask someone to read aloud Exodus 12:1–14 and 26–27. What details about the Passover in these passages stick out to you? What questions do they bring to your mind?

3. Have someone read Mark 14:22–25. What do you think Jesus was saying about the wine representing his blood? Was it merely that wine and blood look similar—or was there something more? And which covenant was Jesus referring to?

4. In Jesus' time, Passover celebrations included wine—a gift their ancestors in Egypt did not have (as slaves, they would have drunk thin beer). The wine reminded God's people they lived in the land of promise, where vines grew in abundance and the hills were flowing with wine. It would have given them hope that God had not forgotten them. How do you see this same principle in the Lord's Supper? What connections do you find?

5. "Wine in the Lord's Supper reminds us that Christ is the choice wine God poured out for the life of the world. He is the noble grape that was crushed in the divine winepress so the world might be reconciled with God and receive everlasting life."[15] Just as grapes are crushed to craft wine, so Jesus died a crushing death to set us free. How does this perspective help you think about Christ's suffering for your sin (both personal sin and systemic sin)? How might that enhance how you partake in communion in the future?

RESPOND | 10 MINUTES

It is fascinating to consider that wine was a healing agent in the ancient world, and that even today it provides us with joy. However, first, the grape must be *crushed* for each of these to be experienced. Think of how this mirrors the life of Jesus, who was crushed for our sins so we may be healed and experience the joy of salvation. As the prophet Isaiah wrote, "He was pierced for our transgressions, he was crushed for our iniquities; the punishment that brought us peace was on him, and by his wounds we are healed" (Isaiah 53:5).

This isn't something to consider just on Lent or Resurrection Sunday but all the time. How does this prophecy speak to the nature of wine and its place in the Christian story?

Just as wine was used as an antiseptic and for healing in the ancient world, so too does Christ's blood cleanse us from sin. It has the spiritual power to heal our relationships and the wounds we carry and inflict on each other. Christ also desires to heal our relationship with food and wine. What are some of the ways that Christ's redemption has healed you, whether that is in personal relationships or your relationship with food and wine? Where do you still desire to see healing in your life, in your community, and in creation?

PRAY | 10 MINUTES

There are various convictions and expressions of communion among different Christian denominations, yet today the sacrament of communion remains a rich, textured, and meaningful experience. Take time in silence to ponder the sacrifice that Christ made for you, your community, and the world. Think about the connection of wine and bread to his blood and body and how we receive Christ's forgiveness and healing. After a few moments of quiet reflection, have a few members of the group share what came to mind for them. When a few people have shared, ask someone to close in prayer by thanking God for this beautiful sacrament of the Lord's Supper and the radically compassionate act of Jesus for our sakes.

SESSION THREE

Personal Study

The Lord's Supper is crucial to the Christian story and to the tradition of the church. "All Christian denominations understand the Lord's Supper as a sacrament. The Lord's Supper is a more constant part of Christian life and worship than are other sacraments, such as baptism."[16] Of course, there are differences when it comes to interpretation. Some denominations believe the bread and wine are the actual body and blood of Christ, while others believe they are a symbolic expression of God's sacrifice through Jesus. Regardless of your tradition, have an open mind this week as you study what the Bible says about this act. Before you begin, take a moment to pray aloud, *"Lord, teach me this week what you want me to know, and let me be free of distractions as I come to your Word."* Once again, record your insights as you go through the exercises. If you are reading *Cup Overflowing* alongside this study, first read chapters 11–15.

When Jesus takes the cup of wine and offers it to his disciples as "the blood of the covenant," he forges a new reality.[17]

PASSOVER TO THE LORD'S SUPPER

By God's grace, most of us will never know what it is like to be enslaved or oppressed, like the Israelites were in Egypt. However, try to imagine for a moment what that must have been like for the nation of Israel to be in Egyptian captivity. They were forced to work against their will in difficult conditions. They were unable to leave or have volition over many of their everyday decisions. They were bound to the decisions made by Pharaoh.

As you consider the physical and relational implications of what this would be like, also consider the spiritual, mental, and emotional problems this would cause. How would you keep from losing hope and dipping into despair? Would you struggle to grasp the goodness of the Lord God you served, the one who had called the nation of Israel to be his special possession? Would you wrestle with God's silence and lack of intervention in your people's lives?

Now consider that as you are working under your Egyptian slave masters, building store cities for Pharaoh like Pithom and Rameses, you hear that Pharaoh has instructed the Hebrew midwives (named Shiphrah and Puah) to kill any newborn male members of your ethnicity. What additional problems would this cause for you in your relationship to God? Would you feel utterly abandoned by him—not so much *chosen* by him but *forgotten* by him?

The Bible doesn't provide us with specific answers to these questions, but we do know that "the Israelites groaned in their slavery and cried out" and that "God heard their groaning and he remembered his covenant with Abraham, with Isaac and with Jacob" (Exodus 2:23–24). God *remembered* them, and he did eventually redeem his people. He did so with a unique set of instructions and commands for his people that involved sacrificing, eating, and being physically ready to flee at a moment's notice.

READ | Exodus 12:1–14

REFLECT

1. Before you dive into this passage, first take a moment to reflect on the Israelites' situation in Egypt. Why do you think God allowed his people to endure slavery and oppression for so long before interceding on their behalf? Why does God continue to allow tremendous suffering around the world, such as human trafficking (a modern-day form of slavery)? How do we hold in tension the reality of suffering and our belief that God is loving and merciful?

> The LORD said to Moses and Aaron in Egypt, "This month is to be for you the first month, the first month of your year. Tell the whole community of Israel that on the tenth day of this month each man is to take a lamb for his family, one for each household. . . . Take care of them until the fourteenth day of the month, when all the members of the community of Israel must slaughter them at twilight. Then they are to take some of the blood and put it on the sides and tops of the doorframes of the houses where they eat the lambs. That same night they are to eat the meat roasted over the fire, along with bitter herbs, and bread made without yeast. . . . This is how you are to eat it: with your cloak tucked into your belt, your sandals on your feet and your staff in your hand. Eat it in haste; it is the LORD's Passover" (Exodus 12:1–3, 6–8, 11).

2. Underline practical instructions that God gives in this passage. How many did you find? Which of the instructions, if any, did you find confusing or perplexing?

> "On that same night I will pass through Egypt and strike down every firstborn of both people and animals, and I will bring judgment on all the gods of Egypt. I am the LORD. The blood will be a sign for you on the houses where you are, and when I see the blood, I will pass over you. No destructive plague will touch you when I strike Egypt. This is a day you are to commemorate; for the generations to come you shall celebrate it as a festival to the LORD—a lasting ordinance" (Exodus 12:12–14).

3. In this passage, circle what God said he would do if the Israelites followed his instructions. If the people were wondering what God meant by "the Lord's Passover," they had their answer. How do you think you would have reacted when you learned an angel of death was going to be sweeping through the land?

4. Notice in Exodus 12:14 that God says, "This is a day you are to commemorate. . . . you shall celebrate it as a festival to the LORD." Why do you think God cared so much in this case that his people remembered and celebrated this event (for all the generations to come as well)? What would be the consequences if the Israelites forgot this act of God and refused to celebrate this divine act of deliverance?

5. Consider the connections between the Passover story and what Jesus said during the Lord's Supper that he was going to do for the world. In addition to the fact that Jesus celebrated this meal at Passover, what other connections and similarities can you find (for example, there was eating and drinking, or a sacrifice was made)?

PRAY | Focus on the experiential nature through which God wanted the Israelites to experience redemption. He didn't just say they would leave when he said so—he gave them practical things to do and experience before that redemption took place. Ask that God would also help you experience him meaningfully, personally, and communally this week—with your whole being: heart, soul, mind, strength, and all your senses. If you are experiencing a season of suffering, or want to identify with someone else who is suffering, consider eating something bitter to help you pray to God in the midst of that suffering. If you are longing for God to intervene in your life, fast for parts of a day. If you experienced a new level of freedom and trust in your relationships, maybe bake some bread or cookies and share it with that person as an expression of gratitude. If you helped clean up a waterway, thank God for giving us fresh water to quench our physical thirst. Include as much as you can of your senses (especially touch, taste, and smell) in your prayer life.

THE PRECIOUS BLOOD OF CHRIST

During the Last Supper, Jesus held the cup of wine and said, "This cup is the new covenant in my blood, which is poured out for you" (Luke 22:20). Today, we are going to explore the topic of blood and its significance in the Bible. Maybe you're comfortable with seeing blood, or maybe you feel a bit light-headed at the thought. Regardless, blood has some amazing properties that make it a unique life source in the world and in our bodies.

The human body contains about five quarts of blood (around 7–8 percent of a person's total body weight). Blood consists mostly of plasma (55 percent), with the remaining amount (45 percent) being red blood cells, white blood cells, and platelets. Blood contains small amounts of metal such as iron, manganese, zinc, lead, copper and even a small amount of gold (about 0.2 milligrams). Blood travels through the body's roughly 60,000 miles of blood vessels, which is long enough to circle the globe more than twice. The heart pumps the equivalent of 2,000 gallons of blood each day. Bloodwork is one of the primary ways physicians can diagnose a person's health.

The ancient Israelites, of course, did not know all these fascinating qualities of blood. However, they recognized that blood was significant. In the Hebrew mind-set, blood was the center of life, both physically and spiritually. It became a symbol of life that had its origin in God and therefore belonged to God alone. This is why, in the Old Testament, the Israelites were forbidden to consume blood. It was always carefully drained from the animal and either poured over the altar or into the soil as a gesture to return it to God, from whom all life comes.

There are almost 400 references to blood in Scripture. As you reflect on today's passages, keep these ideas about the meaning of blood in the Bible at the forefront of your mind. Remember that blood was seen as the center of life and belonged to God alone.

READ | Leviticus 1:1–5; 1 Peter 1:1–7, 13–16; 2:1–21; 3:8–11; 4:8–11

REFLECT

 1. In Leviticus 1:1–5, the Israelites were commanded to sacrifice animals to God at the temple (or tabernacle before the temple was built). The animal sacrifices were a vehicle of prayer—reminders that God, in his justice, needed to punish evil, sin, and injustice in order for the life he intended his people to have to flourish once again. The sprinkling of the blood visualized how God removes the cascading consequences of evil and sin from all spheres of community life (mistrust, revenge, hatred, greed, hopelessness, and the like) so his love and forgiveness could flow freely once more. The temple was a microcosm of God's good creation, and atonement of sins was not understood as merely the forgiveness of individual sin but also the healing and restoration of his deeply broken creation. Why was blood such a powerful symbol for the Israelites? What would all the shedding and sprinkling of blood over the altar have done to their understanding of God and how he atones for us?

2. First Peter picks up the Old Testament temple imagery of blood sprinkled over the altar and applies it metaphorically to speak of Christ's blood sprinkled over believers (see 1 Peter 1:2, 19). Peter emphasizes the benefits of Christ's blood go *way* beyond what we could imagine. In Christ, God has made us into a new people, and our hope now lies hidden with him and his resurrection power, no matter what we experience (see verses 3–7). This living hope is stored up for us in heaven, and *no one* can take it away. Stop and image this kind of hope. Where do you struggle to imagine and cling to this kind of living hope you have in Christ that will never perish?

3. In 1 Peter 1:13–16, the apostle calls us to be "disciplined" and set our hope on the grace that Christ offers. Where do you find it difficult to receive grace and forgiveness? Where are you shackled in one way or another (by shame, fear, anger, worry, and the like) and cannot receive God's grace? In what areas do you need Christ's resurrection power—which alone sets you free and enables you to live a holy life?

The life of the early church was challenging because Christians often experienced persecution. However, this did not deter them from gathering for the *agapē* feast and the Lord's Supper, eating and drinking in each other's homes with real food and real wine, not thin wafers and a tiny sip of wine or grape juice as we do today. It was a more sensuous affair, bringing some comfort and joy into lives marred by persecution and profound suffering. Wine remained a staple and Christians enjoyed wine in their religious celebrations, family feasts, and everyday life whenever possible.[18]

4. Jesus shed his own blood for our salvation and offered us resurrection life so we can be empowered to live life as God intended it (see 1 Peter 1:18–19). As God's people, we are set apart to reflect God's holiness in this broken world. We are set free so we can be obedient to Christ (see 1 Peter 2:16). Look up the following passages and list some of the actions we are called to as "the royal priesthood."

Passage	Actions we are called to as a "royal priesthood"
1 Peter 2:1–5	
1 Peter 2:9–10	

Passage	Actions we are called to as a "royal priesthood"
1 Peter 2:13–17	
1 Peter 2:20–21	
1 Peter 4:8–11	

5. Peter understood that believers were enduring intense persecution for their faith. However, rather than allow this to drive them apart, what does Peter say they should seek to do (see 1 Peter 3:8–11)? What would it look like if believers in Christ today truly embraced this idea and always sought to repay "evil with blessing"?

PRAY | Prayerfully read the following lines from the hymn "I Love Your Kingdom, Lord" by Timothy Dwight (1800). End with a prayer of gratitude to Jesus for paying the price for your sins with his blood. Thank him for giving you a community of like-minded believers who also understand the price Jesus paid and who are also seeking to lead holy lives. Ask that he would continue to help you lean into these relationships during trials.

I love your kingdom, Lord,
the house of your abode,
the church our blessed Redeemer saved
with his own precious blood.

I love your church, O God:
her walls before you stand,
dear as the apple of your eye
and graven on your hand.

For her my tears shall fall,
for her my prayers ascend;
to her my cares and toils be given,
'til toils and cares shall end.

Beyond my highest joy
I prize her heavenly ways,
her sweet communion, solemn vows,
her hymns of love and praise.

Jesus, our Friend divine,
our Savior and our King,
your hand from every snare
and foe shall great deliverance bring.

Sure as your truth shall last,
to Zion shall be given
the brightest glories earth can yield,
and brighter bliss of heaven.

Study 3

CONNECTING THE DOTS

When some people hear the phrase "The Last Supper," their minds immediately go to Leonardo da Vinci's famous painting located in the Santa Maria delle Grazie church in Milan. (Take a moment to look it up online if you are not familiar with the work.) As beautiful and iconic as that piece may be, it can make Jesus seem distant, stoic, and impersonal. We have to be careful to not lose the reality of just how personal and intimate that meal was between Jesus and his disciples. This particular supper, like all meals shared with close friends, would have been filled with conversation, retelling the stories of God's deliverance, and meaningful interactions.

Often, we approach learning something new with a "collect the dots" mind-set, when what is actually needed is "connect the dots." Of course, we can't connect the dots if we don't first collect them, but we have to take that next step in searching for the important connections. With this in mind, think of some of the key connections we've explored this week: the Passover, the life-giving properties of blood, and Jesus with his disciples at the Last Supper.

Today, we are going to keep "connecting the dots" by exploring a story that, again, might be familiar to you. We will also look at a passage that is quoted in some church traditions when the congregation partakes in communion. Before you begin, either pour yourself a glass of wine or have a bottle of wine with you, as you will use this visual for one of the exercises.

READ | Matthew 26:20–29; 1 Corinthians 11:23–26

REFLECT

1. Before you jump into this passage, think about Jesus and the disciples sharing the Last Supper together. "Look" around the room in your mind's eye. What do you notice? What kind of activity is taking place? What kind of conversation is happening among the disciples? What do you picture Jesus saying and doing before he addresses the disciples?

When evening came, Jesus was reclining at the table with the Twelve. And while they were eating, he said, "Truly I tell you, one of you will betray me."

They were very sad and began to say to him one after the other, "Surely you don't mean me, Lord?"

Jesus replied, "The one who has dipped his hand into the bowl with me will betray me. The Son of Man will go just as it is written about him. But woe to that man who betrays the Son of Man! It would be better for him if he had not been born."

Then Judas, the one who would betray him, said, "Surely you don't mean me, Rabbi?"

Jesus answered, "You have said so." (Matthew 26:20–25)

2. Underline the disciples' reactions and Judas's reaction when Jesus said that one of them would betray him. What do you imagine the disciples might have been thinking when Jesus made this statement? What do you imagine Judas was thinking?

> While they were eating, Jesus took bread, and when he had given thanks, he broke it and gave it to his disciples, saying, "Take and eat; this is my body."
>
> Then he took a cup, and when he had given thanks, he gave it to them, saying, "Drink from it, all of you. This is my blood of the covenant, which is poured out for many for the forgiveness of sins. I tell you, I will not drink from this fruit of the vine from now on until that day when I drink it new with you in my Father's kingdom." (Matthew 26:26–29)

3. Look at your glass or bottle of wine. Think about the visual similarities between wine and blood: the color, the viscosity, and the like. What might this visual illustration from Jesus have conjured up in the heads of his disciples? Remember from yesterday's study that the Jewish people were forbidden from drinking or consuming blood because it was the seat of life and belonged to God (see Leviticus 17:10–12). Given this, Jesus' statement to "drink from it" would have been a radical departure from their tradition. What do you think they would have made of this?

4. Jesus went one step further when he said, "This is my blood of the covenant, which is poured out for many for the forgiveness of sins." Remember that forgiveness happened at the *temple* where the priests were in charge. What was Jesus saying about the disciples' need to break with a belief and tradition their families had been steeped in for centuries? What would it have taken for the disciples to accept this and follow Jesus at this moment?

> The Lord Jesus, on the night he was betrayed, took bread, and when he had given thanks, he broke it and said, "This is my body, which is for you; do this in remembrance of me." In the same way, after supper he took the cup, saying, "This cup is the new covenant in my blood; do this, whenever you drink it, in remembrance of me." For whenever you eat this bread and drink this cup, you proclaim the Lord's death until he comes. (1 Corinthians 11:23–26)

5. Circle the similarities in this passage between what Paul reports Jesus saying at the Last Supper and what Matthew reports Jesus saying in the passage you've been studying from his Gospel. What do *you* need to remember when it comes to the sacrifice that Jesus made through his blood on your behalf and on behalf of those you walk with? Why is it so important for you and your fellow believers in Christ to remember Jesus' sacrifice by frequently partaking in communion together—by allowing your senses of smell and taste to help you remember?

PRAY | The Lord's Supper should remind us that Jesus is the "choice wine" God poured out to save us from our sins. Jesus is the noble grape who was crushed in the divine winepress so the world might be reconciled with God. Keeping this in mind, and with your eyes looking at the wine in the glass or a bottle, consider Jesus as the noble grape, God's unimaginable giving of Himself so we can be set free from all that shackles us. Speak honestly and openly to God about what you have experienced in this time. Maybe you've been reminded of something, or made a connection you hadn't seen before, or have become aware of a sin in your life that you need to confess. Or maybe you just are overcome with gratitude for Jesus' sacrifice. Whatever is on your heart, speak it out simply and honestly to the Lord.

CONNECT AND DISCUSS

Consider planning an evening where you gather together with some of the members in your group to discuss the past week's study and to participate in receiving communion. Depending on your church tradition, this may require you to invite your pastor, another ordained minister, or your priest to join you. Ask the members you invite to bring a snack to share that would pair well with wine (cheeses, meats, breads, and crackers work well), and make sure there is wine. Ask everyone to review their notes from the past week on the Passover meal, Christ's blood, and the Last Supper. Then use the questions below to help guide a time of discussion before you actually partake of communion together.

- How are you viewing (1) the Passover meal differently, (2) blood in a new way, or (3) the Last Supper with fresh eyes? Have each person state at least one thing that he or she has learned.

- Where are you confused, curious, or perplexed by what you've studied this far? (If a pastor, ordained minister, or priest is able to join you, ask them to share their perspective and what the communion elements mean to them personally.)

- Do you believe you will experience communion differently moving forward based on what you've learned in this session? Why or why not?

In some traditions, communion is called the Eucharist, from the Greek word *eucharistia*, meaning "giving thanks."[19] So as you end your time, give thanks to God by partaking in the Lord's Supper. You may even do this as the early church did: Let the Lord's Supper overflow into a meal shared with wine to enhance this experience of remembrance.

As you do, savor the smell and taste of the bread—don't chew and swallow it too quickly. Smell the wine first and then take a good sip. Swirl it around in your mouth and allow it to remain there a while before you swallow it slowly. Allow your olfactory receptor cells and taste buds (most of what we think of flavor is actually smell) to experience the multitude of subtle smells, tastes, and sensations that unfold not only in your nose and mouth but also in your whole body. Give your brain time to process the different sensations. Notice what kind of memories surface and what emotions are evoked in you by savoring it.

Remember, savoring wine is a profoundly personal experience. When we smell and taste a wine, we engage in a multisensory experience. In the act of smelling, we draw on the memories of flavor that we've stored in our brains, and these memories, in turn, connect us to more comprehensive memories and emotions we hold in our bodies. As memories surface and emotions are evoked, they inform and shape our conversations, our creativity, and our celebrations. They can deeply impact a whole gathering as the pleasure centers of our brains respond with joyous triggers, stimulating us toward conviviality and festive playfulness.

Finally, when you've all concluded, gather in a warm embrace (if you are comfortable in doing so) and say the Lord's Prayer together aloud.

CATCH UP AND READ AHEAD

Use this time to complete any study and reflection questions that you were unable to finish over the past week. Make a note below of any questions that still linger. Reflect on any new insights or awareness you've gleaned as well as any areas of growth you are discerning.

Read chapters 6 and 20–23 in *Cup Overflowing* before the next group session. Use the space below to make note of anything that stood out to you, encouraged you, or challenged you.

WEEK 4

BEFORE GROUP MEETING	Read chapters 6 and 20–23 in *Cup Overflowing* Read the Welcome section (page 70)
GROUP MEETING	Discuss the Connect questions Pour a glass of wine and watch the video for session 4 Discuss the questions that follow as a group Do the closing exercise and pray (pages 70–74)
STUDY 1	Complete the personal study (pages 77–80)
STUDY 2	Complete the personal study (pages 81–85)
STUDY 3	Complete the personal study (pages 86–89)
CONNECT AND DISCUSS	Get together and watch the film *Babette's Feast* Discuss the follow-up questions (page 90)
CATCH UP AND READ AHEAD (BEFORE WEEK 5 GROUP MEETING)	Read chapters 7–10 and 16–19 in *Cup Overflowing* Complete any unfinished personal studies (page 91)

BREAKING BREAD AND DRINKING WINE

Life Around the Table

*Quick! . . . Bring the fatted calf and kill it. Let's have
a feast and celebrate. For this son of mine was dead
and is alive again; he was lost and is found.*

LUKE 15:22–24

WELCOME | READ ON YOUR OWN

When you hear the word *table*, a few images might spring to mind. Perhaps you picture a table in a conference room where you have meetings with your coworkers. Or maybe you envision a table in a workshop where you put together your craft projects. Or perhaps you think of that table in your home where you and your family play games.

Tables come in different shapes and sizes and are used for all kinds of purposes. However, in its most traditional sense, the table is the place where you eat a meal. Often this is done alone, as you only have time for a "quick bite." But the *best* times around the table happen when meals are shared. Just think of the fun, excitement, frivolity, and—yes—*drama* that occurs around the table when you gather with a group of friends or family.

Certainly, you can enjoy food on the go without a table. Yet there is something about sitting around a table that makes the act more intentional. The table can be a vehicle that encourages *interaction* and builds *relationships* with others—something that goes beyond the act of consuming food! Maybe this is why the Bible contains quite a few references to tables and meals. So much of Jesus' ministry revolved around sharing meals with saints and sinners, rich and poor, high-powered celebrities and forgotten outcasts.

In this session, we will explore the role of wine in extending hospitality—a deeply spiritual act that everybody in the biblical world was called to practice. Hospitality is about opening your home and heart, sharing your resources, and welcoming friends and strangers alike with openness and generosity. We will see that wine and fellowship around the table can help us join in God's mission to love and feed others and make them feel included. We will find that good things happen when we enjoy good food and wine together!

CONNECT | 15 MINUTES

Get the session started by choosing one or both of the following questions to discuss:

- What is something that spoke to you in last week's personal study that you would like to share with the group?

— *or* —

- On average, we eat twenty-one meals a week. Take an inventory of your meals from the past week. With whom did you share these meals?

WATCH | 25 MINUTES

Pour a glass of wine for everyone who is comfortable having one and then watch the video for this session. Below is an outline of the key points covered during the teaching. Record any key concepts that stand out to you.

OUTLINE

I. Life around the table shows up frequently in the pages of the Bible.
  A. Hospitality, the table, and sharing meals are frequent themes (consider Abraham and Sarah, Jacob and Isaac, the Passover, and the Lord's Supper).
  B. Eating with others was a significant part of Jesus' ministry.
  C. Some of these meals were joyous occasions; at others, Jesus confronted the hypocrisy of religious leaders; and at some, Jesus lifted up the downtrodden.

II. Hospitality and eating around the table are key themes in the Gospel of Luke.
  A. Luke's Gospel contains nineteen accounts of meals, thirteen of which are unique to his account.
  B. This is why some call the book of Luke "the gospel of hospitality."
  C. As we probe into these meals, we see that Jesus highly valued life around the table. It was around the table that he laid out some of his most significant teachings.

III. The table allows us to turn our home into a place for the kingdom of God.
  A. Christians used to see gathering around tables as part of their sacred calling.
  B. Hospitality is a lost spiritual practice that we need to reclaim for our time.
  C. Jesus said we should "invite the poor, the crippled, the lame, the blind" (Luke 14:13).

IV. It is at the table in fellowship where Jesus is revealed to us.
  A. Luke tells of two of Jesus' followers traveling to Emmaus (Luke 24:13–14).
  B. Jesus appeared and explained the Scriptures to them, but they didn't get it (Luke 24:15–27).
  C. It was only when the men invited Jesus to stay with them and sat down for a meal that they finally got it—and recognized he was Jesus (Luke 24:28–32).

V. These "table stories" in the Gospels connect with our story.
  A. All meals have the potential to become places of encountering Christ.
  B. The first church gathered around a table to share a meal (Acts 2:46).
  C. The dinner table is a key element in holding families, communities, and societies together. They shape who we are and teach us what it means to live together.

NOTES

_____
_____
_____
_____
_____
_____
_____
_____
_____
_____
_____
_____
_____
_____
_____
_____
_____
_____
_____
_____

DISCUSS | 35 MINUTES

Discuss what you just watched by answering the following questions.

1. There are many stories in the Bible of people sharing meals. What are some significant meals around the table that stand out in your life? How has sharing food and drink (including wine) around the table played a part in building community with others?

2. Luke recorded nineteen meals in his Gospel—nine at which Jesus was present. Shared meals were an important way that Jesus taught and enacted the kingdom of God. The lowly, the sinners, and the social outcasts received a heartfelt welcome and were fed in body, mind, and spirit. Can you name a time when you were invited to someone's table and it had a significant impact on you? What made it so impactful?

3. Ask someone to read Acts 2:42–46. "The breaking of bread" was something the early followers were committed to doing together—in addition to listening to the apostles' teaching and engaging in fellowship and prayer. What stands out in this passage about how they ate together? What happened when they committed to being with one another, fellowshipping around the table, and serving one another?

4. Sadly, for the first time in human history, many families today no longer eat together. What might be some of the barriers that keep people from eating together with friends, family members, coworkers, and neighbors (and maybe even other people we know from church) more often? What would it take to overcome some of those barriers— whether they are logistical, relational, or cultural? What would have to change for *you* to practice hospitality to a greater degree by sharing meals with others?

5. The early church practiced what was called an *agapē* feast, and in the early days, it often included the Lord's Supper. Ask someone to read aloud 1 Corinthians 11:17–22. Why do you think Paul was so adamant in correcting the abuses that were taking place around the table in this congregation? Why was it so easy for the early church in Corinth to slip into wrongful and unjust behavior as they gathered to share meals?

RESPOND | 10 MINUTES

It is at the table where we open our lives to others. We discover that eating and drinking are not just functional activities but are also deeply spiritual and formative practices—nourishing our bodies as well as our minds and souls. Sadly, for many, the common meal around a communal table has all but disappeared. Yet this raises some important questions:

> What if families and communities made the common table the central piece of furniture in the home once more? What if we were to relegate the television and/or the computer to a small corner of the house and restrict the time spent in front of it? Our daily need for food and drink might again become a daily opportunity to turn eating and drinking into a spiritual practice—one in which we learn to open our lives to God and to one another. We have to relearn to discern between physical, emotional, and spiritual hunger and how they can be nourished in different ways.[20]

What might this look like in your immediate family? What are the challenges? What might be the benefits in the short term and long term?

As you dream a bit there and think about this as a possibility, what thoughts come to mind and what emotions do you feel? Does this prospect excite you? Make you anxious? Leave you indifferent? Explain your thoughts and feelings.

PRAY | 10 MINUTES

Close by asking God to give each person opportunities to engage in times of fellowship through the food, drink, and interactions that occur around the table. Pray that God would send guests your way and provide for those future meals: not just for basic sustenance but also for conviviality, laughter, and conversations that lead to comfort, healing, and connection. Finally, pray a blessing over your group host for that person's hospitality.

SESSION FOUR

Personal Study

When it comes to our faith, God encourages us not to just *know* more but also to *experience* more. Food and drink, especially wine, shared around a table can help us experience God's goodness not only through fellowship with others but also by prompting us to engage with all our senses, including taste and smell, which we don't draw on as often in our pursuit of spiritual things. This week, be intentional about picking a table where you will do each day's study. Think about the conversations you have already had at that table—the interactions you've had with others and the kind of food and wine you have savored together. Or if the table is in a public space (like a coffee shop), think about the kinds of conversations that have happened there and what conversations could happen there in the future. As always, record your impressions, questions, and insights as you go through this study. If you are reading *Cup Overflowing*, first review chapters 6 and 20–23 in the book.

Wine and food are gifts that
God can use to bring a Christian
community back together.[21]

INCLUDING OTHERS AT THE TABLE

Perhaps when you think of Zacchaeus the tax collector, that oh-so-familiar children's song immediately pops into your mind:

Zacchaeus was a wee little man, and a wee little man was he.
He climbed up in a sycamore tree, for the Lord he wanted to see.

We often think of Zacchaeus's small stature and what happened in the tree as Jesus passed by. But we rarely give as much attention to what happened when he came down from that tree. In fact, this is the most significant part of the story—and it all happened around a table in Zacchaeus's home.

Now, to us, this does not seem like a big deal. After all, we eat in each other's homes all the time. However, in that day, for an upstanding Jewish man like Jesus to eat in the home of a tax collector like Zacchaeus was a *huge* deal. Who you shared a meal with said a great deal about who you were as a person—your standing in society, your values, and your priorities. This is why all the people who witnessed the event muttered, "He has gone to be the guest of a sinner" (Luke 19:7). Jesus was associating himself with Zacchaeus.

Why did this create such an uproar among the Jewish people? One of the reasons is because tax collectors were viewed as one of the *worst* possible professions that a Jewish man could have. Tax collectors compromised their faith by working *for* the oppressive Romans. They collected taxes for the Romans from their own Jewish kin, even overcharging them so they could skim off a good bit of money for themselves. And Zacchaeus was a *chief* tax collector, which meant he oversaw that whole lot of infidels! Tax collectors were rich, but it was dirty money, and everybody knew it.

Despite all this, Jesus singled him out. He called him by his name and invited himself to dinner at Zacchaeus's house—just like that. How did Jesus know his name? Have you ever wondered about that? Take a closer look at the story.

READ | Luke 19:1–10

REFLECT

1. Read this story from the perspective of Zacchaeus. What do you think he was feeling as he was perched in the tree—or when Jesus called his name and invited himself to come to his home? Do you think he was surprised Jesus knew his name? What would your reaction have been to Jesus' invitation?

2. Now read the story from the perspective of one of the people in the street. Most of them would have been diligent followers of God who worked hard at being faithful to him, obeying his commandments, and not associating with sinners of morally questionable behavior. And had Jesus not just judged a wealthy man who indulged in his riches but could not be bothered to care for his poor neighbor Lazarus (see Luke 16:19–30)? Given the information you just read about tax collectors in first-century Jewish society and Jesus' judgment on rich people who didn't care for the poor, why would it have been so surprising to see Jesus go to Zacchaeus's home?

3. Now read the passage one last time from the perspective of the disciples. As you do, remember that people would have associated you and your standing in society with the rabbi you followed. What would you be feeling as a follower of Jesus, watching him with a fellow Jew who had betrayed his God and God's people? What questions would you have asked Jesus after he returned from having eaten and stayed at Zacchaeus's home, especially since Jesus had just judged rich believers in the story of the rich man and Lazarus?

> When life is busy and you feel worn down, it is tempting to let [hospitality] slip. . . . But hospitality has always been fundamental to the life of the church, and it is a fairly recent development that it is not a common practice anymore. We need a renewed vision to see that hospitality and feasting are powerful ways to be the body of Christ and witness to the life that God has given us to share with the world.[22]

4. In our modern context, inviting ourselves to someone's home would seem presumptuous and even rude. But in the first century, eating at someone's house was a powerful gesture of welcome, acceptance, and bonding. Not everyone welcomed Jesus into their home, and many people were suspicious of or even outright hostile toward him. But Zacchaeus *did* welcome Jesus. He had heard of him and was eager to get a glimpse of this prophet who performed miracles, healed the sick, and fed the poor. What do you think was going through Zacchaeus's mind as he made preparations for the dinner? Was his whole family there? What conversations did they have? (As a traveling itinerant prophet, Jesus might have even spent the night!)

5. It is almost certain that Zacchaeus "would have provided a banquet for Jesus with only the best food and wine."[23] As a wealthy man, he probably had a really good wine cellar. Can you imagine Zacchaeus going down to that wine cellar and picking out a choice wine of exceptional quality and beauty? The whole experience of sharing an extended meal must have been amazing because at the end of it Zacchaeus had a radical change of mind. What does Luke tell us was the overall impact of this meal that he shared with Jesus? What did Jesus declare had come to the "house" of Zacchaeus (see verses 8–10)?

PRAY | The trajectory of Zacchaeus's life changed because he responded to Jesus' request of hospitality. He opened his home to host an itinerant prophet. Zacchaeus's life changed because he got to sit down with Jesus and share an extended meal around a physical table—eating delicious food and choice wine, and knowing that Jesus accepted and loved him. Think about the table you are sitting at right now. Thank the Lord for the life-change that has happened in you because of people reaching out to you, including you, and accepting you around tables like this, just as Jesus did with Zacchaeus. Ask that you would also be an instrument that God would use to include others. Ask that the Lord would give you courage to bring others to your house and to your table as a gesture of welcome and generosity and, through it, to extend to them a heartfelt welcome into Christ's kingdom.

JESUS' PRESENCE AROUND THE TABLE

Have you ever been in a difficult situation and wondered why it felt like God was absent? Maybe you thought that he didn't care to be involved in your life or that you had done something to warrant him giving you the cold shoulder. But later, you realized that he was, in fact, present in the situation the entire time—you just didn't recognize it in the moment. This is often the case when it comes to our perceptions of God. He has a penchant for showing up and being present with us, but we often don't see him.

The story you are going to explore today is a familiar one, but it still might puzzle you. It concerns two followers of Jesus who had left Jerusalem just after Jesus' burial. They were taking the road to a village called Emmaus (see Luke 24:13–35). As they trekked along, they talked about what had happened over the past days and how their hopes had been dashed. There were rumors Jesus had risen, but they didn't really know what to make of them.

From this side of the Easter story, it is easy to assume that everything was wonderful after Jesus was raised from the dead. Yet many of his followers were still fearful, terrified, perplexed, and felt hopeless. The thought of Jesus rising from the dead seemed like idle talk, wishful thinking perhaps (see verse 11). So just imagine what these travelers were feeling as they walked down the road. Their teacher had been killed in the most brutal and humbling way possible: on a cross at the hands of their Roman oppressors. How would you have felt in that situation? Confused? Grieving? In disbelief? All the above?

Suddenly, seemingly out of nowhere, Jesus started walking alongside them, though they didn't recognize him. Jesus didn't reveal his identity to them right away. In fact, more than once, he chose to be naive in his interactions (see verses 17, 19, 28). They recounted all that had happened in Jerusalem, but they still did not realize it was Jesus. As they neared the village, these confused pilgrims invited this "stranger" to stay with them.

There are times when Jesus is present but we don't recognize him in the moment. Instead, we realize it after the fact—maybe when we are sharing a meal with others around the table. Only then are our eyes opened, and we finally realize that Jesus was always in our midst.

READ | Luke 24:13–49

REFLECT

1. These discouraged Jews walked with Jesus for miles along the road as he explained, "beginning with Moses and all the Prophets" (verse 27), what the Scriptures had said about him and his suffering. And yet, even after this intensive Bible study, the men didn't recognize him or understand the meaning of his suffering. It was only when they invited him to stay with them—when they extended hospitality to a seeming stranger—that something happened. As they gathered around the table, Jesus suddenly took on the role of the host: He took bread, blessed it, broke it, and gave it to them. It was then that something was revealed to the two men—and they suddenly recognized him! This simple meal became a place of revelation. Why do you think it was right at this point that the men recognized Jesus? What implications might this have on how Jesus is recognized around the "tables" in your world?

This story in Luke and its implications are about the practice of extending hospitality to strangers and how the breaking of bread has revelatory power. In this instance, the seemingly ordinary breaking of bread at Emmaus is connected powerfully to the extraordinary event of the Lord's Supper. So we see that ordinary meals derive meaning from the ritualistic meal of the Eucharist and can become places of revelation. It is the event of breaking bread that is powerful. Theologically, this is an important point that many Christians today don't make. How many of us see any relation between our daily meals and the Last Supper? Yet here, Luke emphasizes that the *extraordinary* meal of the Lord's Supper now informs *ordinary* meals such as the one at Emmaus. They are profoundly interwoven and connected.

2. As noted in this week's teaching, "What's important here is that the language [of Luke 24:30] is reminiscent of the words Jesus spoke at the Lord's Supper a few days earlier with his disciples. This shared meal becomes a place of *revelation*. They finally understand the Messiah had to die and be resurrected for the kingdom of God to come." Compare the language used in Luke 22:19 with Luke 24:30 (see also Matthew 26:26 and Mark 14:22). Notice the similarities between the two accounts:

Luke 22:19	Luke 24:30
he took bread	*he took bread*
gave thanks and broke it	*gave thanks, broke it*
and gave it to them	*and began to give it to them*

Why do you think the wording of Luke 24:30 resonates so closely with the words of Jesus in Luke 22:19, where he celebrated the Last Supper with his disciples?

Somehow, these shared meals and their meanings are connected. They are not the same, yet the meal at Emmaus and its revelatory power is connected to the Lord's Supper. Consider how the extraordinary meal of the Lord's Supper could imbue your daily life with more meaning than you previously thought. How does this make you think about the relationship between seemingly ordinary meals and what you experience when you partake of the Lord's Supper during Sunday worship?

Are there any other connections you could make between what you experience on Sunday and what is your seemingly "ordinary" life—especially in the way you eat food and drink wine?

3. Jesus had challenging words for these travelers who just could not make sense of his suffering and death: "How foolish you are, and how slow to believe all that the prophets have spoken!" (verse 25). It sounds like they had a real argument, wrestling with spiritual realities that are hard to grasp. They revisited Scripture, and Jesus helped them read the Bible in new ways. After all this, are you surprised they were so adamant that Jesus stay with them? Would you be willing to offer hospitality to someone who challenged your lack of understanding—or would you tend to withdraw into the privacy of your own thoughts and avoid any kind of discussion?

What might this story have to say about the importance of having open discussions and maintaining hospitality in our culture today?

4. Jesus' next post-resurrection appearance was to his disciples—startling and frightening them with his presence (see Luke 24:36–37). Jesus showed them his hands and his feet, but some of them still did not believe. So Jesus then asked, "Do you have anything here to eat?" (verse 41). Jesus may have been hungry, but it is more likely that he was proving a point: Ghosts and apparitions do not eat. Luke then writes, "He took it and ate it in their presence" (verse 43). Why was this detail important for Luke to include in this story?

We haven't been taught the long-term value of sharing a meal and conversation at dusk; most people, therefore, believe that shoving a high-calorie, processed fast-food item down our throats while riding in a seven-passenger vehicle accomplishes the same end. It doesn't. We were born with the need to unpack our day within a circle of people who know us and deeply care about us. When we exchange this kind of simple existence for a motion-obsessed existence—which takes lots of discretionary money to pull off—new evils and new illnesses are birthed in our homes and in our bodies. Simply put, when our relationship time is unbalanced, life doesn't work.[24]

5. In Luke 24:36–37, Jesus demonstrated to his followers that he had risen in the flesh by allowing them to touch his wounds and by expressing physical hunger. He asked for food, and his disciples then shared a meal with him as an expression of resurrection life. Here, Luke brings to a climax the theme of the importance of meals in Jesus' ministry—before *and* after the resurrection. In fact, Jesus makes his resurrection presence known to his followers *by sharing a meal* with them at a table—not once, but twice. Consider how we have lost this practice in our culture. What do you see as the long-term value of sharing a meal with others? What steps can you take, and what priorities can you shift, to make room for meals around the table?

How can you make others more aware that Jesus is with us when we share meals and that the food we eat and the wine we enjoy are gifts from God to nourish us physically, emotionally, and spiritually?

PRAY | Assuming you are at the same table as you were during the first personal study, take a moment to be still and reflect on your physical setting. Write a brief prayer (two to four sentences) to thank God again for the work he has done around the table before you. Also ask the Lord to do a new thing in your life—to surprise you with his presence around the table, even if you do not immediately recognize that it is Jesus who is with you!

A GENEROUS CHRISTIAN LIFE

In the Gospels, we find stories of Jesus eating meals with his disciples (see Matthew 26:17-21); or with close friends like Martha, Mary, and Lazarus (see Luke 10:38-42); or even with those on the fringe of society (see Mark 2:13-17). However, in the story we will read today in Luke 7:36-50, we find Jesus dining in the home of someone we might not expect: a *Pharisee*. The Pharisees were religious teachers who claimed the Torah as their authority, and in the Gospels, we usually find them questioning, criticizing, or condemning Christ. However, this Pharisee, named Simon, invited Jesus to dine at his home, and Jesus accepted.

Meals were often where Jesus enacted and taught about the kingdom of God, and this meal was no different. While the setting is the home of Simon, the focus quickly shifts to a woman who shows up uninvited. In doing so, she was likely taking advantage of social norms that permitted those in need to visit banquets like the one Simon was hosting to receive some of the leftovers. However, it was still a bold and radical move on her part. This woman had a reputation for being a sinner in that village, yet she still came to the home of a Pharisee.

The woman had heard about Jesus and saw something in him that gave her hope and courage. She brought what must have been one of her most precious possessions and offered it as a sacrifice of sorts. She knew that she was a sinner, but she also recognized that Jesus had come from God and could help her. She wept at the feet of Jesus, washed them, dried them, kissed them, and then anointed them with her expensive oil from an alabaster jar. The fragrance of that oil would have filled the room with powerful and pleasant aromas.

We can only wonder what impact this moment had on those who were present at the meal. It must have been powerful. Certainly the host, Simon, reacted strongly to this radical and sensual gesture of humility and generosity—but not in a positive way! It is quite likely that, even years later, whenever they smelled the scent of the oil the woman poured on Jesus' feet, they returned to this point in time. In so doing, they could reminisce about what they had witnessed on that day and what Jesus had revealed about the kingdom of God.

READ | Luke 7:36-50

REFLECT

1. Take a moment to engage with the scene in Luke 7:36–50. First picture Simon the Pharisee, a respectable Jew with his family and guests reclining with Jesus at the table. Jesus had upset the religious status quo and become a threat to Israel's religious leaders, and yet Simon was curious enough to invite Jesus to dine with him. What do you think Simon was hoping for? What did he want to learn?

2. Now consider the scene in Luke 7:37–38. The woman might have been a prostitute. How do you picture her as she enters the room? Does she linger for a while behind Jesus before she acts? What smells fill the room as she opens the alabaster jar?

How do you think the woman felt when she kissed Jesus' feet and wiped them with her tears? What might she have felt as she poured one her most precious possessions over Jesus' feet? How do you think Jesus felt in this moment?

It should not be surprising...that Jesus spent so much time eating and drinking with people, many of them outsiders and on the fringe of society, lacking respectability. It was a mark of his ministry to share their joys and their sorrows as he dipped his bread in olive oil and sipped wine from the cup offered to him as a sign of hospitality. That did not always sit well with the religious establishment. No wonder they accused him of being a glutton and drunkard (Matthew 11:19; Luke 7:34).[25]

3. Simon, who was well versed in studies of the Torah and Jewish purity laws, witnessed these actions taking place and was deeply troubled. Simon knew this woman was impure. He said to himself, "If this man were a prophet, he would know who is touching him and what kind of woman she is" (Luke 7:39). Simon's complaint was that Jesus should have also known this woman was impure and kept himself pure by touching her. Can you see Simon struggling between his traditional understanding of the law and what Jesus taught? Do you sometimes struggle between traditional Christian teaching and new ethical realities you face?

4. Simon, in spite of his struggle and confusion, still calls Jesus a teacher (see verse 40). In true rabbinic form, Jesus then teaches Simon by telling a story (see verses 43–43). How might this story have helped Simon move forward?

Notice the upside-down nature of what Jesus continues to do in his ministry. After telling the story, he compares Simon's perhaps meager hospitality to the humble, serving, and sacrificial actions of the woman (see verses 44-47). How might Simon have felt hearing this? How might the woman have felt after being compared to such a high-standing and respectable teacher of the law?

When Jesus ushers in the kingdom of God, he introduces an upside-down vision of how God acts in this world. Jesus has come for all humanity to be redeemed and restored into a new family. The table now becomes a primary place where we gather as this new community—where social groups (like families) open up to others and social boundaries are dissolved. We are called to break out of isolation and loneliness and learn to feast together as a way of being children of the living God. So let's learn to open our homes once more to express God's hospitality and welcome those whom Jesus might send our way. Some of those guests might be surprising and even difficult, but in this way, we participate in God's healing and restoration of a deeply broken humanity.

5. Jesus was willing to eat and drink with a wide variety of people: sinners, social outcasts, and those of low social status (such as Zacchaeus and the sinful woman). He also ate and drank with religious leaders and those in powerful social and political positions (like Simon). How does the way Jesus interacted with people around the table challenge you? What does generosity look like when it means to embrace those who are forgotten, sidelined, and seemingly undeserving?

Can you imagine your table as a place where Christ becomes the host for building his kingdom? Why or why not?

PRAY | As you end in prayer, think about the relationships in your life. Think of those in your life who are in need of a healing or comforting touch from Jesus right now. Ask that God would give you a more generous heart to be willing and able to meet those needs.

CONNECT AND DISCUSS

The film *Babette's Feast* (1987) provides a beautiful depiction of what it means to savor and enjoy the gifts of food and wine that God has provided and what it means to live a generous and even sacrificial Christian life.[26] Just as the sinful woman in Luke 7 offered up a sacrificial gift of precious oil, so Babette—a poor and long-time refugee with a newfound fortune—offers up her gifts to help restore unity among a divided Christian community. The film also captures how conviviality gains momentum and how the gifts of hospitality, food, and choice wine transform a divided and uptight religious group of people into a merry party.

Consider planning an evening to watch the film with those from your group. (You can easily find the film online for a minimal rental fee.)[27] You may also want to consider sharing a meal together beforehand where everyone brings one of their favorite dishes to share and wines that match the food (you can easily search online for which foods go with particular wines). If you can't get together to watch the film with your group members, make a commitment to watch it with family members or friends. Note that this is a slow-paced film, so don't expect an action movie. The film is rich in visualizing the movement of God's grace when people gather and share a carefully prepared meal.

If watching the film is out of the question, at least make the attempt to gather together for a meal to discuss the following questions. If you can't do a full meal, consider putting together a charcuterie board of meats, cheeses, olives, fruits, bread, and wine.

- If you could host a feast like Babette, what would you serve? Who would you invite? What would you hope would happen around the table during the meal?

- What is one thing you learned this week, either from the video or from your personal study, about the importance or significance of wine around the table?

- Which part(s) of the film moved you the most? Why was it so moving for you?

- Based on what you've learned, watched, discussed, and studied thus far, how might the engagement of your senses, which God has graciously given to enjoy him and his world more fully, help you appreciate more of who God is?

- How has this week's material encouraged you to seek out others to join you around the table? What value do you now see in sharing meals together?

CATCH UP AND READ AHEAD

Use this time to complete any study and reflection questions that you were unable to finish over the past week. Make a note below of any questions that still linger. Reflect on any new insights or awareness you've gleaned as well as any areas of growth you are discerning.

Read chapters 7–10 and 16–19 in *Cup Overflowing* before the next group session. Use the space below to note anything that stood out to you, encouraged you, or challenged you.

WEEK 5

BEFORE GROUP MEETING	Read chapters 7–10 and 16–19 in *Cup Overflowing* Read the Welcome section (page 94)
GROUP MEETING	Discuss the Connect questions Pour a glass of wine and watch the video for session 5 Discuss the questions that follow as a group Do the closing exercise and pray (pages 94–98)
STUDY 1	Complete the personal study (pages 101–103)
STUDY 2	Complete the personal study (pages 104–107)
STUDY 3	Complete the personal study (pages 108–111)
CONNECT AND DISCUSS	Connect with one or two group members Discuss the follow-up questions (page 112)
CATCH UP AND READ AHEAD (BEFORE WEEK 6 GROUP MEETING)	Read appendix 1 and 3 in *Cup Overflowing* Complete any unfinished personal studies (page 113)

WHAT DID THE SAINTS DRINK
The Tale of Two Wine Drinkers

Go, eat your food with gladness, and drink your wine with a joyful heart, for God has already approved what you do.

ECCLESIASTES 9:7

WELCOME | READ ON YOUR OWN

One of the great benefits in being part of a community of Christ-followers known as the church is that we have the opportunity to learn from those who have gone before us. We have writings and stories from faithful followers of Jesus that demonstrate how we can also be faithful to Christ. We also have the stories and examples of those who led lives of foolishness and disobedience to Christ that we can take as a warning.

Church history can be a helpful tool to assist us in learning from those brothers and sisters who have gone before us. We are, as one writer put it, "surrounded by such a great cloud of witnesses" (Hebrews 12:1). These models of the faith include not just individuals found in the Bible—like Paul, or Peter, or James—but also the monks and nuns, bishops and pastors, and authors and martyrs that are so influential in our collective history.

Some have the opinion that looking at church history is boring and irrelevant. Yet if we give these women and men a chance, they will inspire us across the centuries by reminding us of what is most important and showing us how to live with wisdom, intentionality, and purpose. While these women and men were not perfect, their stories can give us a clearer glimpse of the overarching story of God and what he is doing in our world.

Now, when we consider these saints of the faith, we tend to look at what they prayed, studied, wrote, or preached. We don't often think about what they *drank*. However, the saints—both those from centuries past and still living—had much to say about wine. In this session, we will explore the lives of some of these followers of Jesus and what they can teach us about how to have an appropriate relationship with wine in our lives.

CONNECT | 15 MINUTES

Get the session started by choosing one or both of the following questions to discuss:

- What is something that spoke to you in last week's personal study that you would like to share with the group?

— *or* —

- What comes to mind when you hear the word saint? Was this language something that was a part of your faith tradition growing up?

WATCH | 25 MINUTES

Pour a glass of wine for everyone who is comfortable having one while watching the teaching and then watch the video for this session. Below is an outline of the key points covered during the teaching. Record any key concepts that stand out to you.

OUTLINE

I. Wine has enjoyed a long and rich history in the life of the church.
   A. The views of Christians on wine has changed over the centuries.
   B. In fact, it was only after Thomas Welch applied pasteurization to grape juice that some denominations stopped drinking wine.
   C. Before this time, *all* Christian denominations used wine in the Lord's Supper.
II. Our personal stories impact how we view drinking wine and alcohol.
   A. Gisela—who grew up on a winery in Bavaria, Germany, and attended a Lutheran Church—never experienced resistance to wine until moving to America.
   B. Randy—who grew up in Cleveland in a home where alcohol was abused and a church that forbade it—didn't experience receptivity to wine until later in life.
   C. Regardless of our own stories, wisdom and the proper perspective can help us learn to embrace wine appropriately, wisely, and joyously.
III. The fact is that many people have traumatic experiences around alcohol.
   A. A culture can—and should—develop wisdom and guidelines around how to enjoy wine and alcohol in ways that are wholesome, life-giving, and sustainable.
   B. To develop a more wholesome relationship with wine, we first have to heal, which can take a long time (sometimes, it might take a couple of generations).
IV. Church history reveals we can have an appropriate relationship with drinking wine.
   A. For centuries, wine was farmed and fermented under the guidance of the church—especially the Benedictine, Cistercian, and Franciscan monks and nuns.
   B. Benedict of Nursia, who penned the *Rule of Saint Benedict*, said that every monk and nun could drink one *hemina* (about two glasses of wine) per day.
   C. The Protestant Reformers drank and defended the enjoyment of wine.
V. Wine has a place in our community, society, and church today.
   A. It is time we reclaimed wine as a gift from God and pondered how to embrace it.
   B. We must reclaim the spiritual practice of gathering around the table. It's in community we learn wine's place in our faith, feasting, and fellowship.

NOTES

_____
_____
_____
_____
_____
_____
_____
_____
_____
_____
_____
_____
_____
_____
_____
_____
_____
_____
_____
_____
_____

DISCUSS | 35 MINUTES

Discuss what you just watched by answering the following questions.

1. As you have undoubtedly discovered, people in the church come from a variety of backgrounds and experiences. As you listened to the teaching, whose personal story—Gisela's or Randy's—did you resonate with the most? If someone were to ask you to briefly share what your story is as it relates to *wine*, what would you tell them?

2. Only after Thomas Bramwell Welch (the founder of Welch's Grape Juice Company) applied pasteurization to grape juice in the late nineteenth century did some Christian denominations stop drinking wine. Before that, *every* denomination used wine during communion. How does knowing that history impact how you view the use of wine in the universal church—and within your local church?

3. Ask someone to read aloud Ephesians 5:18. There has been considerable effort, particularly in the United States, to convince people that the wine in Bible times wasn't fermented—that it was just some form of grape juice. How do passages like this one from Paul prove that this cannot be the case? Based on what you have learned in this study, how would you now respond to someone who claimed that wine in the Bible was just grape juice?

4. Martin Luther famously wrote, "Wine and women bring sorrow and heartbreak, they make a fool of many and bring madness, ought we therefore to pour away the wine and kill all the women? Not so."[28] What point was Luther making here? Where does the problem lie when it comes to overindulgence in wine—with the wine itself or with the person who abuses it?

5. "Perhaps you feel slightly sinful for indulging in a glass of wine or overly afraid that wine might be the devil's tool of temptation. Whatever your background might be, the beautiful and mysterious worlds of wine and faith never should have been severed from one another."[29] What would it look like—in your life, in your circle of friends, in your church—to reclaim the mindset that wine is a *gift* from God?

RESPOND | 10 MINUTES

Reflect on this idea of reclaiming wine as a spiritual gift from God and embracing it appropriately in the midst of your community. Consider this truth:

> The Bible invites us to enjoy wine in the community of the saints, not as lone rangers or in the secrecy of our homes. God's gift of wine calls us into the community that is the body of Christ. . . . I encourage you not to get into the habit of drinking by yourself, or if you have already established this habit, try to wean yourself of it. Join a group that enjoys wine and experience how wine savored in community has the benefit of helping you feel more connected in a playful and relaxed way. Conviviality is a powerful antidote to loneliness and the isolation that many of us feel.[30]

Conviviality simply means to have joyous celebration in the company of others. Can you think of examples in the Bible where conviviality is present? Why do you think conviviality is highlighted with such frequency in the pages of the Bible?

When have you engaged in God-honoring conviviality with wine? What was that experience like for you? Are there opportunities to plan for some conviviality in your group or with others in different settings in the future?

PRAY | 10 MINUTES

Take a moment to think of those you know who do not routinely experience *conviviality*—those who struggle with loneliness and isolation. Silently pray for each of them. Then, as a group, thank God for the times of joyful connection that you've experienced as you savored and relished food and wine and enjoyed the company of others. Ask the Lord if there are ways you could invite others to join you for a time of savoring food and wine, meaningful conversation, joy, and yes—conviviality.

SESSION FIVE

Personal Study

We all have different stories when it comes to wine. For some, wine has always been something to be cherished and enjoyed. For others, wine is filled with pain and trauma. Then there are those who have been taught that drinking wine is wrong. However, as we've seen, wine has a frequent presence in Scripture, and has been in the lives of the church for centuries. This week, you will explore what your relationship is to wine and how it might be used for good in how you love and care for others. So, as you engage in these studies, have your eyes open, your noses ready to smell, and your taste buds attuned with a view toward sharing God's gifts of the earth with others. Once again, record your thoughts, questions, and insights as you go along. Also, if you are reading *Cup Overflowing*, first review chapters 7–10 in the book, which will give you a great background to the history of wine in the church, and chapters 16–19, which will provide you with insights on alcohol use and abuse.

Some need not drink. For the rest of us, the challenge is to develop a healthy and wholesome relationship with wine.[31]

Study 1

PRACTICING THE "ONE ANOTHERS"

While we as believers in Christ share many things in common, we have different approaches to church-oriented issues, including communion, baptism, worship, liturgy, and wine. We also face divisions in our Christian communities due to politics, our attitude toward money, and the various cultural backgrounds and values we embody. We live in a wonderfully diverse culture, and our vocation as Christians is to build bridges where we can.

While Jesus calls us to draw the line on issues related to sin or heresy, there can and should be a healthy diversity of convictions held by Christians. The gospel calls us to work toward unity of the Spirit and break down barriers where possible, just like Jesus did with Zacchaeus in Luke 19 and the sinful woman in Luke 7. There is nothing more Christlike and disarming than sharing a beautiful meal with those who are different from us. We can let the gifts of delicious food and fragrant wine do their work in us and among us.

One of the purposes of this *Wine in the Word* study has been to help you uncover the many benefits and blessings of wine and see that it can be gladly received as a gift from God. Yet it is also important to recognize that not everyone sees wine this way. As shared earlier, many people have been wounded by the effects of alcohol abuse by a family member or friend. Some struggle with addictions themselves. Others come from a background where drinking alcohol was not tolerated and thus can't see drinking wine as anything other than wrong. Others are just not ready to see wine as a gift.

With this in mind, it's important that we treat these differences and disputes among believers with patience, compassion, and understanding. As Jesus said, we are to first and foremost "love one another" (John 13:34). Paul, in many of his epistles, likewise encouraged us to engage in several "one anothers" by loving, serving, and accepting those in the body of Christ. Peter did the same in his letters. In fact, there are more than fifty "one anothers" found in the New Testament!

Today, the goal is for you to explore how you and those in your group can love "one another" in spite of any differences—even your differences of conviction about wine.

READ | 1 Corinthians 1:10–17; Romans 12:9–16

REFLECT

1. Based on Paul's words to the believers in 1 Corinthians 1:10–17, it is apparent that differences of opinions in the church have existed for centuries. What was the problem causing division in this church? What was Paul's remedy for the problem?

> Love must be sincere. Hate what is evil; cling to what is good. Be devoted to one another in love. Honor one another above yourselves. Never be lacking in zeal, but keep your spiritual fervor, serving the Lord. Be joyful in hope, patient in affliction, faithful in prayer. Share with the Lord's people who are in need. Practice hospitality. Bless those who persecute you; bless and do not curse. Rejoice with those who rejoice; mourn with those who mourn. Live in harmony with one another. Do not be proud, but be willing to associate with people of low position (Romans 12:9–16).

2. Read this passage aloud. What do you hear as you read? What line, phrase, or sentence stands out to you? Write that line, phrase, or sentence in the space below.

3. Go back to the passage and underline all the times that Paul says "one another." What main instructions do you find when Paul mentions these "one anothers"?

4. Focus on verse 10: "Be devoted to one another in love. Honor one another above yourselves." Think of someone you know who holds different theological convictions than you do. Next, personalize the verse by inserting their name:

"I will be devoted to _____ in love. I will honor _____ above myself."

Now make this even more personal by writing some of the *specific* ways you can be devoted to this person in love and honor him or her above yourself.

5. Finally, think about these verses as they relate to people's views on wine. What does it mean to be devoted to that person in love despite your differences (see verse 10)? What does it mean to practice hospitality with those who do not share your views (see verse 13)? What does it mean to live in harmony with them (see verse 16)?

PRAY | End by praying in three parts. First, keep the names, faces, and stories of the people you've thought about during this study at the forefront of your mind. Pause and pray briefly for each one by name. Second, spend focused time praying for yourself. Maybe you need to ask for forgiveness for the way(s) you haven't honored others. Share that with the Lord. Third, boldly yet humbly ask the Lord to grant you the wisdom, patience, and compassion to practice the "one anothers" through the power of the Spirit this week—with those you listed and everyone with whom you come into contact.

Study 2

GUIDED BY WISDOM

Wisdom from God is certainly needed when it comes to alcohol use. Kate Julian, a journalist and senior editor for *The Atlantic*, wrote, "A little alcohol can boost creativity and strengthen social ties. But there's nothing moderate, or convivial, about the way many Americans drink today."[32] Some, such as authors Holly Whitaker and Annie Grace (both recovering alcoholics), have responded to the unhealthy drinking patterns they see in America with a call for people to not drink alcohol at all.[33]

But such a stand should cause us to pause. For those who are recovering alcoholics, it might be best to abstain. But for those who do not struggle with addiction, there is a more biblical way forward. As we discussed, in Psalm 104:14–15 we read that God "[brings] forth food from the earth: wine that gladdens human hearts." If wine is a gift and blessing from God that gladdens our hearts, why would he want us to completely abstain from it?

A much better approach is to seek God's wisdom when it comes to consuming wine. We must ask, *What can a healthy and wholesome drinking culture look like?* The beginning of wisdom is to develop a healthy sense of awe, wonder, reverence, and respect for who God is and what he has given us. The book of Proverbs, as we have learned, compares the pursuit of wisdom to a wise woman who prepares a feast that is accompanied by mixed wine. Like the enjoyment of a carefully and generously prepared feast, we are called to seek out and enjoy the wisdom we need to flourish in this life (see Proverbs 9:1–6). Proverbs celebrates wine as a precious gift from God. We are to enjoy wine in moderation and abstain from excessive and abusive drinking habits—including drunkenness.

Now is the time for us to explore our own relationship with wine and how to develop wisdom, rituals, practical guidelines, and boundaries around our enjoyment of it so we can contribute to the growth and development of a healthy drinking culture in our midst. We are called to take the steps that are necessary to help us develop a drinking culture where wine is appreciated and celebrated rather than misused and abused. So let's devote this next personal study to seeking wisdom for our enjoyment of wine together.

READ | Titus 2:3; Galatians 5:19–21; 1 Corinthians 5:11; 6:10; John 2:9–11

REFLECT

 1. As you begin this study, take a moment to reflect on the local culture in which you live. How would you describe the attitude you find toward drinking alcohol? What do you observe in local supermarkets or at children's parties, football games, golf tournaments, concerts, fundraising events, church gatherings, and the like when it comes to consuming alcohol?

What kind of alcohol is consumed there, and at what time of the day? Is drinking and driving considered a concern?

Do you feel pressure to drink when you are not comfortable in doing so? Are there boundaries in place when it comes to wine and alcohol consumption? Would you consider the overall approach to be healthy, unhealthy, or both?

The prophet Isaiah rebukes wealthy rulers who amass possessions and oppress the poor and spend entire days indulging in wine, feasting to excess (Isaiah 5:8–12; 28:1, 3). Paul, who ministered in pagan contexts where drunkenness was often permissible or even encouraged, has little patience with it. He admonishes a group of older women on the island of Crete to give up heavy drinking and practice moderation instead (Titus 2:3). He challenges the believers in Galatia to stay away from drunkenness (Galatians 5:19–21) and even encourages the church in Corinth repeatedly to stay away from those given to alcohol abuse (1 Corinthians 5:11; 6:10).[34]

2. The New Testament continues the wisdom of Proverbs and condemns alcohol abuse and drunkenness. Reflect on your life and those you share it with: family, friends, acquaintances, and colleagues. Use the following questions to really ponder your habits and write them down. If you don't feel comfortable sharing all of them that is okay—the important step here is to bring awareness to yourself and others.

What patterns and practices do you see that might be healthy and wholesome? Which ones might raise concern?

When do you start drinking? How much do you drink, how often, and what kind of alcohol?

How often do you share a glass of wine, and how often do you drink alone?

Do you tend to drink wine and alcohol when you are stressed or lonely, or do you drink it with others and in the context of a meal?

3. North America has had a unique and tumultuous relationship with alcohol (mostly distilled spirits and beer) that has included pendulum swings between overindulgence and abstinence. Have you ever traveled to a country and observed habits and practices that exhibit a healthy drinking culture? How could you learn from countries like Italy and Spain, where the primary drink is wine—and has been for thousands of years?

4. In order to develop a healthy drinking culture, we need to talk more openly about it. We need to have the courage to talk about our history with alcohol and how to develop a more wholesome drinking culture. Do you feel comfortable beginning such a conversation? Why or why not? (See appendix 1 to help you begin.)

5. The wedding feast of Cana, the Lord's Supper, and the meals and feasts mentioned in the Bible teach us that wine is a gift and blessing from God that can enhance our feasts and celebrations and help us forge deeper bonds with each other. It is a powerful way to defy the despair, hopelessness, and loneliness in our midst. What are your favorite feasts and celebrations? Do you enjoy wine as part of the feasting?

Feasting together used to be much more prevalent in society as a way to live out one's faith and bring people together. How could you help bring your community together more often to celebrate?

PRAY | As you conclude this study, reflect on what you sense God is communicating to you about the appropriate use of wine and alcohol. Express to him any concerns that you have. Finally, pray that God would continue to help you and your community to take steps toward developing a more healthy and wholesome drinking culture.

Study 3

SAVORING GOD'S GIFT WITH GRATITUDE

We have come a long way in understanding the gift of wine God has given us. Wine is a gift from God's good earth, and its beauty and quality are shaped by the particular place in which vines grow. God placed into nature this incredible potential for fruitfulness and beauty. It is not a product of human work, yet it impacts a wine's quality in unique ways.

Wine's quality and beauty, however, are profoundly shaped by the divine-human collaboration that many vintners will attest to as a humbling reality. Often, vintners view themselves as mere midwives of a vintage: tending to vines and grapes, harvesting, ensuring a safe fermenstation, blending wines, and properly storing wine for aging to allow a vintage to evolve and mature. Those who craft wines are therefore—from a biblical perspective—not *wine makers* but *vintners* (or, as the French put it, *vignerons*, vinegrowers). This divine/human collaboration is itself a beautiful and challenging dance.

Wine has the potential for incredible beauty—a beauty that connects the attentive drinker to the place *and* culture where it was crafted. This connection to a particular place and its culture is part of its beauty. Wine has the potential for great complexity, depth, and bountiful variety in color, bouquet, taste, texture, structure, and composition. It takes time and effort to become attentive to this often subtle beauty in a wine.

The beauty that wine offers takes us into the rhythm of death and resurrection. Each vintage undergoes a process of transformation from grapes that experience a kind of "death" by being crushed and pressed to grape juice that ferments into a beautiful and fragrant wine. And if it is red and fortified wine, it speaks profoundly to Christ's blood. What other food can speak so powerfully of Christ's death and resurrection and our participation in it?

Wine is a gift of beauty that brings joy. We enter into the joy that God has given us as we gather together, celebrate, and savor wine. As a thoughtfully given gift, fragrant wine and delicious food develop their own dynamic and draw us into their orbit as conviviality grows and gathers momentum. Here, joy is no longer the feeling or experience of an individual. Rather, it deepens as we share it and allow it to draw us together. No wonder wine has served as a social lubricant for centuries! Let us receive this gift with reverence and gratitude.

READ | Ecclesiastes 2:24–25, 3:9–14, 5:18, 8:15; Song of Songs 1:2; 2:4

REFLECT

1. It is in our daily and ordinary lives that we are called to draw near to God and cultivate gratitude and joy. In Ecclesiastes, we are called to reflect on our ordinary lives and the importance of enjoying it. Cooking, eating, and sipping a glass of wine together is meant to bring us pleasure and joy even in the midst of jobs that we might not enjoy. To reject or neglect this invitation to enjoy the simple pleasures of life is to ignore the Giver of life and refuse to honor him and the life he provides. What feelings do the passages from Ecclesiastes that you read evoke in you? How can you learn to recover the enjoyment of simple pleasures?

The Song of Songs stands in a long tradition of erotic love poems, and writers throughout the ages have continued to celebrate wine and sex as wonderful gifts to humanity. . . . The Song of Songs celebrates sex, like wine as a gift from God with such natural grace and vivid imagery that it makes the stoic blush and the ascetic deny its literal meaning. What is so beautiful about the Song of Songs is that it is smack in the middle of the Bible and thereby embeds the enjoyment and delight of sex and wine into the journey of faith.[35]

2. The Song of Songs celebrates sex as a gift from God and compares it to the enjoyment of wine (see 1:2). These are fundamental and sensuous gifts given to humanity, and the Song of Songs celebrates and highlights their importance. What is your response to this idea? How does it make you feel?

What does this add to your understanding of wine?

3. Song of Songs 2:4 literally reads, "He takes me into his wine cellar/house of wine and his banner of me is love." Why do you think contemporary Bible translators have replaced "wine cellar" with "banquet hall" (as in the New International Version)?

Does this passage make you think of the wedding feast of Cana or Jesus speaking of himself as the bridegroom? How do you feel about thinking of your relationship with God as a great love affair?

4. In some Orthodox churches, it is tradition to put on a feast for the young women and men when they turn sixteen, eighteen, and twenty-one. They are served delicious food and wine, and each year the celebration gets more lavish. It is one way the mature believers prepare the younger women and men to understand wine as a gift from God and learn to enjoy it. How can you help a younger generation understand wine as a gift from God and learn how to enjoy it rather than abuse it?

5. Historically, the church has looked on eating and drinking through the lens of the vice/virtue paradigm and contrasted gluttony with temperance. Temperance focuses on our ability to restrain ourselves but leaves little room to actually enjoy food and wine as God intended it. What if we instead contrasted gluttony with *savoring*—and elevated it to a Christian virtue? Savoring is the thoughtful and slow enjoyment of food and wine. It includes temperance but goes beyond it, for it encourages us to actively seek out the beauty we find in food and wine. In what ways would the act of savoring be a better contrast to gluttony?

How do you feel about savoring as a spiritual pursuit? How do you think savoring could lead you to find more joy in the everyday things of life?

PRAY | As you close this study, pray the words of Psalm 104:14–15 as an act of praise to the Lord: *"God, thank you for giving us the plants of the earth to cultivate, so that we can bring forth good food from the earth. Thank you also for the gift of wine, which gladdens our human hearts, and for all the other gifts of sustenance that you provide. Amen."*

CONNECT AND DISCUSS

Try connecting with one or two group members this week. While it is recommended that you connect in person, if that is not possible, try to at least connect via phone, text, video conference, or email. When you gather together (in whatever form it takes), use some of the prompts below as a way to engage in conversation together.

- This week, you heard Gisela's and Randy's stories about the attitudes they grew up with concerning wine. Is there anything you've learned this week about your own relationship to wine? What have you learned about other people's stories?

- In the first personal study, you explored some of the "one anothers" found in the Bible. What did you learn during that study? What application(s) did you take away from that time that would be important to share with someone else?

- In the second personal study, you explored the wisdom needed around drinking wine. What are some unhealthy patterns you identified in your culture or your own life? What are some positive ways that can help us all develop a healthier and more wholesome drinking culture in our midst?

- In the third personal study, you learned more about why wine is such a special gift, how it can help you cultivate joy, and about the virtue of savoring. What is one detail, thought, or feeling that emerged as you explored?

- How have the studies this week encouraged you to continue experiencing God through all your senses—taste, touch, smell, hearing, and sight?

CATCH UP AND READ AHEAD

Use this time to complete any study and reflection questions that you were unable to finish over the past week. Make a note below of any questions that still linger. Reflect on any new insights or awareness you've gleaned as well any areas of growth you are discerning.

Read appendix 1 and 3 in *Cup Overflowing* before the next group session. Use the space below to make note of anything that stood out to you, encouraged you, or challenged you.

WEEK 6

BEFORE GROUP MEETING	Read appendix 1 and 3 in *Cup Overflowing* Read the Welcome section (page 116)
GROUP MEETING	Prepare in advance for the wine tasting Follow along with Gisela and Randy as they lead you through wine tasting as a spiritual practice Discuss the questions that follow each tasting Linger in the moment and conclude (pages 116–126)
STUDY 1	Complete the personal study (pages 129–130)
STUDY 2	Complete the personal study (pages 131–132)
STUDY 3	Complete the personal study (pages 133–134)
WRAP IT U P	Connect with someone in your group (page 135) Complete any unfinished personal studies Connect with your group about the next study that you want to go through together

SESSION *Six*

WINE TASTING AS A
SPIRITUAL PRACTICE
An Experiential Learning Journey

He has taken me to the [wine cellar],
and his banner over me is love.

SONG OF SONGS 2:4

WELCOME | READ ON YOUR OWN

As the poet Gerard Manley Hopkins mused, this beautiful world the Lord made "is charged with the grandeur of God."[36] And we, his children, are invited to relearn what it means to savor the world that he has made. There is hidden in creation such astonishing beauty, yet we have lost the art of paying attention. "Getting and spending, we lay waste our powers; and little there is in nature that is ours," wrote William Wordsworth.[37] It is a consequence of the fall that we have lost the ability to truly taste and see nature as God's handiwork.

The psalmist reminds us that nature is imbued with profound spiritual meaning and invites us to join in the continual praise that creation sings to its Creator (see Psalm 104). A choice wine, as we have learned from the miracle of Cana, speaks to us about Jesus and his kingdom. We need to reclaim a sense of wonder for this astonishing creation and, in particular, for wine as a gift from God's beautiful earth. But how do we do this?

In the following exercise of "wine tasting as a spiritual practice," we want to help you savor wine as a spiritual gift and make room for astonishment and wonder in your midst. Before you begin, note this final session is different than the others—and, quite possibly, will be a new experience for you. It's intended to be experiential, fun, and formative for the group. You've watched the video sessions in past weeks all in one sitting, but with this video, you will be following along as we go through a wine tasting as a spiritual practice experience. In order to engage with this, you will want to stop the video at times when instructed.

While this session requires a bit of preparation to provide the items needed for your time together, and a longer time commitment than the other sessions, we hope and believe that through it you will truly experience the gift of wine that God intended it to be—and that you will find it to be meaningful and joyful to share with others in your group. We can't think of a better way to officially end the *Wine in the Word* study than by encouraging you to experience the goodness of God with all of your senses—learning to pay attention to the subtle sensations as you smell and taste different wines and feel them with your body. May you be able to "come to your senses," in the best sense of the word, and may joy overtake your group, allowing you to see that indeed the world is charged with God's grandeur.

PREPARATION FOR THE WINE TASTING

Before you begin the video, make sure you have the following items ahead of time (see also Appendix 2, "Instructions for Holding Wine Tasting as a Spiritual Practice," in this guide).

WHAT YOU WILL NEED

For each person, you will need one or two wineglasses (depending on whether you want to use one for white wine and one for red wine), a water glass, a plate for very simple bread, and a container (spittoon) where guests can pour wine that they don't want to finish. We usually calculate one bottle of wine of each variety for no more than ten people.

TIME COMMITMENT

We recommend that you devote at least two hours to this experience and allow time for lingering for those who can stay and savor the atmosphere created by this wine tasting.

WHAT WINES TO GET

We recommend that you get between four and six different wines for this wine tasting. If you come from a wine region or live close to one, focus on those local wines. If not, work with a local wine shop that offers a wide range of different wines from different regions, with a focus on artisan wines that reflect a particular region. We like to use traditional and easily available grape varieties such as Chardonnay, Sauvignon Blanc, and a Riesling for the white wines and Pinot Noir, Chianti Classico from the Sangiovese grape, Cabernet Sauvignon, Bordeaux blend (Cabernet Sauvignon, Merlot, Cabernet Franc, Petit Verdot, Carmenère and Malbec), or a Côtes du Rhône blend (usually made from Grenache Noir, Syrah, and Mourvèdre) for the reds. Begin with the whites starting from dry to sweet and then move toward red, beginning with the lighter reds and then moving toward the more full-bodied ones. You can start with a sparkling wine if you wish. Serve your guests some water and bread between tasting the whites and the reds to cleanse their palates. Make sure your white wines are chilled before serving.

MOVING BETWEEN VIDEO AND YOUR OWN WINE TASTING

Gisela and Randy will be leading their group through a wine tasting as a spiritual practice experience. Follow their lead and pause the video when instructed so you can focus on your group and the wines you selected. Your group will develop its own dynamic, and your wines will speak to you in unique ways, so it is important to make room for this. The meditations that appear in the Watch section below have been adjusted slightly from both what Gisela and Randy present to their group in the video and appendix 2. Read through them first after you pause the video. They are intended to help you imagine that this wine tasting can and should become a spiritual exercise—and it is important to be reminded of this with each wine. After reading these, and as you taste the wines, give yourself permission to be quiet in order to become attentive to the wines and what you are sensing. Only after doing so share with your group what you are sensing, feeling, and thinking.

WATCH | 40 MINUTES (VIDEO RUN TIME)

As you begin the wine tasting experience, remember the following:

- In the video, Gisela and Randy sample five different wines: two white (moving from drier to sweeter), and three red (moving from lighter to heavier). Sampling around this same number (four to six) will help you notice the differences in the wines and gain confidence that you can explore them on your own terms.
- You will each experience the wines in unique ways because of the flavor memories you have stored up and because each body will respond differently to them. For this reason, pay careful attention to the smells, tastes, textures, and sensations that you experience in your body.
- Between the different tastings, you will want to cleanse your palate with a little bit of water or some bread.

THE FIRST TASTING

Name of white wine you will be sampling: _____

Pour the first wine and start the video.

VIDEO HIGHLIGHTS

- The meditation for this wine is "To Drink is to Pray." This is from a German meditation: *"To drink is to pray, and to binge drink is to sin."* The line between praying and sinning is sometimes very fine, and drinking in moderation is something we want to do on a regular basis. It is the foundation for developing a healthy relationship with wine.

- Simone Weil, a French philosopher and mystic, wrote that attention, taken to its highest degree, is like prayer. In other words, when we gather up all our abilities to be attentive and pay attention to the gifts set before us, it can become a form of prayer. We express our gratitude by our willingness to be attentive. So, as you begin this spiritual exercise, focus your attention on what is before you in the glass.
- Before you begin, keep these important tips for wine tasting in mind:
  - Swirl the wine around in your glass.
  - Place your nose into the glass and smell the wine, and then pause.
  - Smell it again, slowly. Then take a good gulp and move it through your mouth.
  - Let the wine sit in your mouth for a while, and then slowly swallow it.
  - Pay attention to the sensations you feel in your body.
- This might not be easy for you, as our Western tradition has taught us to focus on seeing and hearing and not on smelling, tasting, and savoring. It will be tempting to get distracted and just talk, but try to stay focused and attentive to the subtle aromas that many wines have. Allow each meditation to remind you that this wine tasting is a form of prayer.
- As you drink the first wine, pay careful attention to what you smell and taste. Pause and ask, *What does the wine remind me of? What do I smell and taste? How does it make me feel?* (You could respond with words or with sounds—a grunt, a nod, or an "mmmm . . ."). Give yourself permission to stay silent to pay attention to what you are smelling and tasting.

Pause the video when directed on screen, and then write down your responses to the following questions.

What sensations did you experience when you smelled and tasted the wine?

_____

_____

_____

_____

_____

_____

_____

What is your reaction to the meditiation for this tasting: "To Drink Is to Pray"?

_____

_____

_____

_____

_____

_____

_____

Take a few minutes to share your impressions with one another, keeping an eye on the time. Once you are ready to move on, start the video for the second tasting.

THE SECOND TASTING

Name of white wine you will be sampling: _____

Pour the second wine and start the video.

VIDEO HIGHLIGHTS

- The meditation for this wine is "The Priesthood of All Drinkers." While you can learn from wine experts, often their wine talk will leave you feeling intimidated, and you may be tempted to stop paying attention to what you actually smell and taste and feel. It is important for you to experience the wines on your own terms, drawing on your personal storehouse of flavor memories and allowing the smells to evoke emotions, memories, and past experiences that are unique to you.[38]
- God has given each of us the incredible capacity to smell and taste. The average human tongue has between 2,000 and 8,000 taste buds, and each taste bud has around 150 taste receptor cells.
- We also have millions of olfactory receptor cells, located in our nose, that give us the capacity to smell. Our capacity to smell and taste is an incredible gift from God—yet one that we have to reclaim, as many of us are not accustomed to paying attention to it.
- We have to reclaim savoring as a spiritual practice!

What differences did you discover in terms of smell, texture, and taste between this wine and the previous one?

_____

_____

_____

_____

_____

_____

_____

_____

_____

_____

_____

What is your reaction to the meditiation: "The Priesthood of All Drinkers"?

_____

_____

_____

_____

_____

_____

_____

_____

_____

_____

_____

_____

Take a few minutes to share your impressions with one another, keeping an eye on the time. Once you are ready to move on, start the video for the third tasting.

THE THIRD TASTING

Name of red wine you will be sampling: _____

Pour the third wine and start the video.

VIDEO HIGHLIGHTS

- The meditation for this wine is "The Gift of Holy Tipsiness." We often think about intoxication in purely negative terms. While it is true we don't want to get drunk, there is a level of slight intoxication that is quite beautiful—one that helps us to relax, unwind, and open up. At this level, confessions come more easily: confessions of delight and pleasure but also of loss, defeat, and failures.

- The beauty of holy tipsiness is that it invites us to be honest and let go of any pretenses that we have it all together. It can liberate us to embrace where we are at in our lives and allow others to see us in that place. In fact, one of the most beautiful gifts we can give to each other is permission to be who we are, see where we are, and accept and love one another in that place.

- We can learn together to wait on God and trust him with our lives. Holy intoxication can also free us from worry and anxiety. It can allow joy to rise in our midst and gather momentum into a convivial togetherness. The clinking of wine glasses is the sound of togetherness.

Pause the video when directed on screen, and then write down your responses to the following questions.

What different sensations did you experience as you moved to this red wine?

_____

_____

_____

_____

_____

_____

_____

What is your reaction to the meditiation for this tasting: "The Gift of Holy Tipsiness"?

_____

_____

_____

_____

_____

_____

_____

_____

_____

_____

_____

Take a few minutes to share your impressions with one another, keeping an eye on the time. Once you are ready to move on, start the video for the fourth tasting.

THE FOURTH TASTING

Name of red wine you will be sampling: _____

Pour the fourth wine and start the video.

VIDEO HIGHLIGHTS

- The meditation for this wine is "The Gift of Place." What does it mean for us to be at home in this world—especially since we live in a globalized world where we are free (or sometimes forced) to move around? Many of us ask: *Where is my home? What does it mean to be at home in this world? How do I connect with particular places and their cultural traditions?*
- Wines crafted with thoughtfulness, where the vintners work hard for the wine to reflect the place where it was grown, can help us to connect to that particular place and its culture. These wines can make us feel more at home in this world.
- Here the vintners become like "priests" as they mediate between heaven and earth. They enable the beauty that God has placed into his creation to sing its unique song through the wine we learn to savor.

- Carlo Petrini, founder of the slow-food movement, said we must pay attention to the *particulars of place*. There is rich meaning and history in those places. They protect us from the onslaught of a globalized homogenization of flavors where everything tastes the same no matter where we are (think sodas and fast food).

Pause the video when directed on screen, and then write down your responses to the following questions.

What are some memories that came up for you as you savored this wine?

_____

_____

_____

_____

_____

_____

_____

_____

What is your reaction to the meditiation for this tasting: "The Gift of Place"?

_____

_____

_____

_____

_____

_____

_____

Take a few minutes to share your impressions with one another and allow the convivial spirit to gain momentum. Give yourself over to the experience of joy and savor it. Keep an eye on the time. Once you feel ready to move on, start the video for the fifth wine tasting. Pause where suggested in the video, or watch it until the end for the final prayer. (You can also restart the video and watch the final prayer at the end before you disperse as a group.)

THE FIFTH TASTING

Name of red wine you will be sampling: _____

Pour the fifth wine and start the video.

VIDEO HIGHLIGHTS

- The meditation for this wine is "Wine in the Great Finale." This meditation focuses on *eschatology*, which is the study of the end times. In Matthew 26:29, Jesus says to his disciples, "I tell you, I will not drink from this fruit of the vine . . . until that day when I drink it new with you in my Father's kingdom."
- Whenever we drink wine, we should remind ourselves that we are awaiting the fulfillment of things to come in the future, at the end of time, when Christ will return to be with his bride once more. As Christians, we are a people of hope.
- As we learn in 1 Peter 1:3–5, we have a living hope through Jesus Christ, with an inheritance stored up in heaven that will never perish or fade. In this life we will experience turmoil and hardship, but we are called to live by hope and faith.
- Wine reminds us of Christ's blood and the hope we have in the power of the resurrection. With longing and joy, we anticipate being reunited with the resurrected Christ. Wine is God's way of kissing humanity.

**Pause the video when directed on screen, and then write
down your responses to the following questions.**

Which of the five wines stood out to you in terms of smell, texture, and taste? Why did that particular wine stand out the most?

_____

_____

_____

_____

_____

_____

_____

_____

What is your reaction to the meditiation for this tasting: "Wine in the Great Finale"?

_____

_____

_____

_____

_____

_____

Take a few minutes to share your impressions, continuing to give yourself to the communal experience as you linger in the joy and fellowship you share with each other. If you have a sixth wine, continue from here and add your own reflection.

THE SIXTH TASTING [OPTIONAL]

Name of wine you will be sampling: _____

Write down any sensations you experience or reflections you have in the space below.

_____

_____

_____

_____

_____

_____

A SLOW CONCLUSION

As you continue to savor the wines together, allow joy and conviviality to gather momentum. Linger prayerfully in the present and allow conversations to unfold. Some of the most important connections happen after you have finished the "official" wine tasting. Give yourself permission to linger and remain attentive to what the Holy Spirit might be doing in your midst. Remember, to drink is to pray.

SESSION SIX

Personal Study

We hope you found the wine tasting experience with your group to be meaningful, formative, and filled with joy. Maybe it has given you a more layered and robust experience of and a greater appreciation for the blessing of wine that God has given to his people. The personal studies in this final session consist of three meditations. These will help solidify your learning so it can be ingested—both literally and figuratively—into your everyday life.

Maturity and wisdom in our
faith journey are like a choice wine
aged in God's wine cellar.[39]

Study 1

SAVORING AND WISDOM

In the first wine tasting, Gisela shared this German meditation: "To drink is to pray, and to binge drink is to sin." Drinking wine invites us to listen discerningly to our body, and this helps us connect to the beauty in the wine and engage with it. Gisela mentioned French philosopher and mystic Simone Weil, who argued that attention, taken to its highest degree, is akin to prayer.[40] Simone Weil strongly believed that the beauty we find in nature is an amazing gift from God that he placed there to draw us closer to himself. In a world that is distracted and rushed, tasting wine can help us to focus and slow down to savor, relish, and truly enjoy what we are tasting. But it can also help us to think reflectively about life and shape our conversations with each other. This element of wine tasting is not often discussed or valued in our culture.

1. As you smelled and tasted the wines, what emotions, thoughts, or memories did they evoke in you? How did they shape your conversations? Pray for those with whom you had a meaningful encounter at the wine tasting.

2. We talked earlier in this study about the importance of wisdom and discernment, especially around things like wine and alcohol. Gisela mentioned there is sometimes a fine line between praying and sinning. What are some practical ways you can drink discerningly while also enjoying it joyfully? Be as specific as possible.

3. Think of a time you experienced God's goodness through smell and taste. Maybe it was through freshly ground coffee beans or a lilac bush. Or maybe it was when you tasted your grandmother's favorite dish or the perfectly ripened strawberry picked from the garden. How have you experienced God's goodness is what you've smelled or tasted? Share it below, and then write a prayer of gratitude for God's goodness in tangible, sensorial form.

4. Gisela introduced savoring as virtue. Reflect on how often or little you to pause during any given day to savor something. How could you build small periods of savoring into your day that become a form of prayer infused with gratitude for what God has given you?

Study 2

HOLY TIPSINESS AND THE GIFT OF PLACE

As Gisela and Randy moved to the third tasting, you might have noticed that the wines were moving from lighter to bolder. Gisela used the phrase "holy tipsiness" in this portion of the video. Perhaps this was a bit jarring for you when you heard her use this statement, as the thought of being "tipsy" only holds negative connotations for you. However, as Gisela mentioned, being just slightly tipsy can actually help to loosen us up, allow us to be ourselves, and help us not succumb to the need to pretend or be someone we are not.

1. Who are the people with whom you can entirely be yourself—where you feel known, celebrated, and loved for who you are? At what times are you most capable of allowing other people to be who *they* truly are? Write a prayer below thanking God for these people who allow you to completely be yourself and do not judge or shun you. Ask God to give you the love, grace, and patience to allow others to be who they are.

2. The idea of paying attention and noticing was touched on again in this tasting, as it is an important theme. Gisela encouraged you to stick your nose in the glass and truly smell the elements of the wine—the subtle flavors and aromas. Where might you need to slow down and just *be* and *savor*—especially those times you are most tempted to run off to the next thing on the schedule or address the next thing on the agenda? Ask the Lord to help you move at an appropriate pace—to give you the courage and discipline to slow down—so you can notice the blessings he has made available to you and those you can share them with.

3. In the fourth tasting, Gisela shared the meditation of "The Gift of Place." Some important questions were asked: *What does it mean to be home in the world? Where is home? How do we connect with place?* In our transient and mobile world, it is important to consider the rootedness and place of people, groups, and objects. Context matters. Where someone or something is from has an impact on who or what that person becomes—and wine and food can serve as a guide to help us connect to a particular place. What are your thoughts on this meditation? How do you connect with place?

4. Jesus grew up in Nazareth, which had its own wine processing facility. Jesus' parents, Mary and Joseph, would have at least had wineskins in their cellar. The wine at the wedding feast of Cana (which ran out) would have probably come from a nearby wine region. The wine that Jesus used at the Lord's Supper in Jerusalem might have come from one of the disciples' family vineyards or the family vineyard of their host. Do you have a wine region close by? What grows well where you come from? Have you ever gone to your local farmer's market and talked to the farmers to hear their experiences of growing food? Write down your reflections below

As you end, take a moment to pray specifically for where you live. Thank God for the soil that brings forth food and wine. And thank him for the farmers and growers who work to heal the soil so we all can continue to be nourished by the earth in the future.

HOPE, JOY, AND CONVIVIALITY

The final meditation was called "Wine in the Great Finale." Jesus said to his disciples, "I tell you I will not drink again of this fruit of the vine until that day when I drink it new with you in my Father's kingdom" (Matthew 26:29 ESV). As followers of Jesus, we await the fulfillment of things in the future—at the end of time—when Christ, the Bridegroom, will return to be with his bride once more. As Christians, we are a people of hope.

1. When the Jews celebrated the Passover meal, they reserved one seat with a glass of wine set at the table for the prophet Elijah. It was an act of faith and hope that God would act in the future. When Jesus celebrated the Lord's Supper with his disciples, he promised to drink wine with his followers in the age to come. Gisela mentioned how wine can bring us joy and that joy and anticipation can and should be linked together. As Christians, we can live with hopeful anticipation that we will be reunited with Christ. What visible reminders and practical gestures could you implement in your life and community to actively cultivate hope for the future?

2. Think of how God created humans with the capacity for joy. How is your life different because of the presence of joy and hope? In what situations do you find that joy and anticipation are linked in your life?

3. As your group went through the wine tasting, perhaps you noticed the group dynamics changing over the course of the evening. Try and relive the evening, savoring those moments when you felt joy was gaining momentum into conviviality. What was it like when you were able to linger and just savor the wine and the fellowship?

4. Gisela shared a German saying that "wine is God's way of kissing humanity." Were you able to connect the sensual pleasures of savoring wine and the convivial fellowship with the goodness of God? Where might Jesus be inviting you to experience and share more joy and anticipation in your life and community? How could a deepened sense of hope help to stir joy in your life and community even in subtle ways?

WRAP IT UP

As you conclude this study, connect with a group member during the week and share some of the key takeaways and insights you had from the wine tasting experience. Use any of the prompts to help guide your discussion and interaction.

- What did you enjoy about the wine tasting experience? Which wine did you enjoy the most? Which one did you enjoy the least?

- What did you enjoy the most about your interaction with others?

- In what ways did you benefit from your personal study time this week as you reflected on Gisela's meditations?

- How has your life been changed, shifted, or been formed through this study? Do you now pay more attention to your capacity to smell and taste? How will this study change the way you view wine and the beauty of this earth in the future?

Use this time to go back and complete any of the study and reflection questions from previous days that you weren't able to finish. Make a note of what God has revealed to you this week. Finally, discuss with your group what studies you might want to go through next and when you will plan on meeting together again to study God's Word.

Appendix 1

DISCUSSION GUIDE FOR DEVELOPING A HEALTHY DRINKING CULTURE

Begin a conversation in your family, church family, or the community you feel comfortable with about wine as a gift from God and how to develop a wholesome relationship with it. Over time, different cultures have created some helpful guidelines for the consumption of wine. My (Gisela's) hope is that we can have a wider conversation in North America about this and develop some guidelines that will protect us and give us a safe space in which we can enjoy wine as God intended.

Consider the following suggestions:

- Every time you enjoy a glass of wine, remind yourself that it is a gift from God.
- Drink with other people, and keep enjoying wine alone to a minimum.
- Savor wine slowly; don't drink it too quickly.
- If you are thirsty, quench your thirst with water first, and then drink wine for enjoyment.
- Limit your drinking to one or two glasses per day for women and two to three for men.
- Drink wine mainly in the context of a meal, and learn how to pair wine with food.
- If you do drink hard liquor, whether straight or in a cocktail, drink it sparingly and only occasionally.
- Consider drinking only after 5:00 p.m., unless it is a special day like Sunday and you are enjoying a festive lunch to celebrate the day of rest that God has given us. Other exceptions would include special feasts, such as Christmas, Easter, and Pentecost, and special occasions, such as weddings, birthdays, and anniversaries.

- Try not to drink wine every day, and build in times of fasting from alcohol, such as certain weekdays or seasons like lent or "dry January."
- When you feel stressed, anxious, or worried, call a friend or someone who might be able to help you. Do not reach for wine or alcohol to ease your stress.
- When you are in a season of working through emotional pain, it is better to abstain from wine and alcohol because alcohol can easily detach you from the arduous process of getting in touch with unwelcome and difficult emotions.
- Be careful about drinking alcohol at work and with colleagues. Be cautious about letting your guard down.
- Drink coffee or tea or other nonalcoholic beverages at a children's party to model a restrained life of alcohol consumption.
- Be grateful for those moments when you can pause to savor a glass of wine with others.

Please remember that these are just suggestions; I am not trying to lay down a law here. However, I have found these guidelines to be very helpful, and I hope that they can encourage you to set boundaries to help you develop a joyous and life-giving relationship with wine. Remember, to drink is to pray. Wine was always meant to help us commune not just with each other but also with the giver of all good gifts, God himself.

Appendix 2

INSTRUCTIONS FOR HOLDING A WINE TASTING AS A SPIRITUAL PRACTICE

Note: The wine tasting as spiritual practice presented in this appendix varies slightly from what Gisela and Randy presented to their group in the video for session six.

What you need: For each guest, a wineglass, a water glass, a plate for simple bread, and a container (spittoon) in which guests can pour wine that they don't want to finish.

What wines to get: I (Gisela) recommend that you get between four and six different wines. If you can, work with a local wine shop that offers a wide range of wines from different regions. I like to use traditional and easily available grape varieties such as Chardonnay, Sauvignon Blanc, and Riesling for the white wines, and Pinot Noir, Chianti Classico from the Sangiovese grape, Cabernet Sauvignon, and Bordeaux blend (Cabernet Sauvignon, Merlot, Cabernet Franc, Petit Verdot, Carménère, and Malbec) or a Côtes du Rhône blend (usually made from Grenache Noir, Syrah, and Mourvèdre) for the reds. Begin with the whites, moving from dry to sweet, and then drink the reds, beginning with the lighter reds and moving toward the more full-bodied ones. You can start with a sparkling wine if you wish. Serve your guests some water and bread between tasting the whites and the reds to cleanse their palates.

How much time will it take: Because you want to create a contemplative atmosphere where guests can enjoy and savor not only the wine but also thoughtful conversation and a convivial atmosphere, I recommend spending at least one and a half hours to taste four wines, and at least two hours for six. Create an atmosphere with few distractions, such as music, candles, or flowers. Keep it simple because you want to focus your senses of touch, smell, and taste on the wine. We tend to get easily distracted by visuals and trivial conversations. Allow guests to concentrate on tasting the wine and savoring it.

For each wine you taste, offer a meditation to help your guests embrace the wine tasting as a spiritual practice. Following are the meditations I usually use, and you can add to them or change them as you see fit.

1. MEDITATION FOR THE FIRST WINE: TO DRINK IS TO PRAY

- To drink is to pray, but to binge drink is to sin (a German proverb).
- Simone Weil, a French mystic, said that attention in its highest form is prayer.
- Let us be prayerful as we approach these wines and learn to pay attention to them with our noses attuned to smell and our tongues attuned to taste.

2. MEDITATION FOR THE SECOND WINE: THE PRIESTHOOD OF ALL DRINKERS

- Introduce guests to the concept of the priesthood of all drinkers: We all have been given the capacity to smell and taste, and we need to develop the confidence that we can smell and taste wine on our own terms. Give your guests permission and confidence to do so. Experts can contribute to our understanding but can also be intimidating in how they speak about wine and weaken our confidence.
- God has endowed us with an incredible capacity to taste and smell. The average person has between 2,000 and 10,000 taste buds, and each taste bud has between 50 and 150 taste-receptor cells. We have millions of olfactory receptor cells, and these expand from our noses to the back of our throats and integrate the process of tasting and smelling. Ponder this great capacity and invite your guests to pay more attention to these senses of taste and smell.
- The complexity of flavors in our world is a gift of great abundance, and yet so often it goes unnoticed and moves us not. Give your guests room to be moved and touched by what they touch, taste, and smell. Do not be afraid of silence.

3. MEDITATION FOR THE THIRD WINE: THE GIFT OF HOLY TIPSINESS

- Invite your guests to think about allowing their relationship with alcohol to heal and mature.
- Mention the importance of temperance.
- Gentle intoxication gives us the gift of conviviality.
- We learn to relax a little and let go of our need to hold up a façade, pretending we have it all together.

- Reflect on the gift of providing an atmosphere of trust where guests can put down their masks and pretenses and learn to be vulnerable and receptive.
- To be known for who we are and to experience acceptance and love are among the greatest gifts we can give to one another.
- Reflect on the gift of more intimate and caring community.

4. MEDITATION FOR THE FOURTH WINE: THE GIFT OF PLACE

- Reflect on what it means to be at home in the world.
- Wine helps us to connect to particular places.
- The vintner becomes a mediator between God and place, and facilitates our connection with place. Thoughtful vintners "listen" to the particular places they cultivate and seek to craft wines that reflect the beauty of these places.
- Why this is important: In a globalized world, we need to reconnect with the local and the particulars of this world. Crafting and drinking wines that reflect particular places can help us reconnect with the importance of the local and of paying attention to the local.

5. MEDITATION FOR THE FIFTH WINE: WINE AND THE GREAT FINALE (ESCHATOLOGY)

- Read Matthew 26:29: "I tell you, I will not drink from this fruit of the vine from now on until that day when I drink it new with you in my Father's kingdom" (also found in Luke 22:18).
- Whenever we drink a glass of wine, it should remind us that we still await the fulfillment and completion of all things in the future. We are a people of hope. And this should instill in us a holy restlessness that the fulfillment of things is still to come. Learn to savor wine and cultivate hope for God's future.
- Pray: "Come, Lord Jesus, come and deepen our longing for your kingdom."

6. MEDITATION FOR THE SIXTH WINE: WINE IS GOD'S WAY OF KISSING HUMANITY

- Think about how intimate an encounter it is with God's creation when we sip a well-crafted wine. It can also be an intimate encounter with our Creator God.

As you bring your own reflections to a close, allow the convivial atmosphere to gather momentum and enjoy watching your guests have good conversations, joyous moments, and meaningful encounters with each other, and hopefully also with God.

LEADER'S GUIDE

Thank you for your willingness to lead your group through this study! What you have chosen to do is valuable and will make a great difference in the lives of others. The rewards of being a leader are different from those of participating in a group, and we hope that as you lead, you will discover new insights into the blessing of wine as revealed in God's Word.

Wine in the Word is a six-session Bible study built around video content and small-group interaction. As the group leader, imagine yourself as the host of a party. Your job is to take care of your guests by managing the details so that when your guests arrive, they can focus on one another and on the interaction around the topic for that session.

Your role as the group leader is not to answer all the questions or reteach the content—the video, book, and study guide will do that work. Your job is to guide the experience and cultivate your small group into a connected and engaged community. This will make it a place for members to process, question, and reflect—not necessarily to receive more instruction.

There are several elements in this leader's guide that will help you as you structure your study and reflection time, so be sure to follow along and take advantage of each one.

BEFORE YOU BEGIN

Before your first meeting, make sure the group members have a copy of this study guide. Alternately, you can hand out the guide at your first meeting and give the members time to look over the material and ask any preliminary questions. Also, make sure the group members are aware they have access to the streaming videos at any time by following the instructions provided with this guide. During your first meeting, ask the members to provide their names, phone numbers, and email addresses so that you can keep in touch with them.

Generally, the ideal size for a group is eight to ten people, which will ensure that everyone has enough time to participate in discussions. If you have more people, you might want to break up the main group into smaller subgroups. Encourage those who show up at the first meeting to commit to attending the duration of the study, as this will help the group members get to know one another, create stability for the group, and help you know how best to prepare to lead the participants through the material. If your group is comfortable with having a glass of wine while watching the video, please have that arranged before you begin.

Each of the sessions in *Wine in the Word* begin with an opening reflection in the Welcome section. In sessions 1 to 5, the questions that follow in the Connect section serve as an icebreaker to get the group members thinking about the session topic. In the rest of the study, it's generally not a good idea to have everyone answer every question—a free-flowing discussion is more desirable. But with the icebreaker question, you can go around the circle and ask each person to respond. Encourage shy people to share, but don't force them.

At your first meeting, let the group members know that each session also contains a personal study section that they can use to continue to engage with the content until the next meeting. While doing this section is optional, it will help participants cement the concepts presented during the group study time and help them better understand how God intends for wine to be a blessing and source of joy for his people.

Let them know that if they choose to do so, they can watch the video for the next session by accessing the streaming code provided with this study guide. Invite them to bring any questions and insights to your next meeting, especially if they had a breakthrough moment or didn't understand something.

PREPARATION FOR EACH SESSION

As the leader, there are a few things you should do to best prepare for each meeting:

- **Read through the session.** This will help you become more familiar with the content and know how to structure the discussion times.
- **Decide how the videos will be used.** Determine whether you want the members to watch the videos ahead of time (again, via the streaming access code provided with this study guide) or together as a group.
- **Decide which questions you want to discuss.** Based on the length of your group discussions, you may not be able to get through all the questions. So look over the discussion questions provided in each session and mark which ones you definitely want to cover.
- **Be familiar with the questions you want to discuss.** When the group meets, you'll be watching the clock, so make sure you are familiar with the questions you have selected. In this way you will ensure that you have the material more deeply in your mind than your group members.
- **Pray for your group.** Pray for your group members and ask God to lead them as they study his Word and listen to his Spirit.

Keep in mind as you lead the discussion times that in many cases there will be no one "right" answer to the questions. Answers will vary, especially when the group members are being asked to share their personal experiences.

STRUCTURING THE DISCUSSION TIME

You will need to determine with your group how long you want your meetings to last so that you can plan your time accordingly. Suggested times for each section have been provided in this study guide, and if you adhere to these times, your group will meet for ninety minutes. However, many groups like to meet for two hours. If this describes your particular group, follow the times listed in the right-hand column of this chart:

Section	90 Minutes	120 Minutes
CONNECT (discuss one or more of the opening questions for the session)	15 minutes	20 minutes
WATCH (watch the teaching material together and take notes)	20 minutes	20 minutes
DISCUSS (discuss the study questions you selected ahead of time)	35 minutes	50 minutes
RESPOND (write down key takeaways)	10 minutes	15 minutes
PRAY (pray together and dismiss)	10 minutes	15 minutes

Note: These sections and times do not apply to session 6, which is a unique wine tasting as a spiritual practice experience led by Gisela and Randy. Refer to the notes in that session for a detailed explanation of how to structure that group time.

As the group leader, it is up to you to keep track of the time and to keep things on schedule. You might want to set a timer for each segment so that both you and the group members know when the time is up. (There are some good phone apps for timers that play a gentle chime or other pleasant sound instead of a disruptive noise.)

Don't be concerned if group members are quiet or slow to share. People are often quiet when they are pulling together their ideas, and this might be a new experience for some of them. Just ask a question, and let it hang in the air until someone shares. You can then say, "Thank you. What about others? What came to you when you watched that portion of the teaching?"

GROUP DYNAMICS

Leading a group through *Wine in the Word* will prove to be highly rewarding both to you and your group members. But you still may encounter challenges along the way! Discussions can get off track. Group members may not be sensitive to the needs and ideas of others. Some might worry that they will be expected to talk about matters that make them feel awkward. Others may express comments that result in disagreements. To help ease this strain on you and the group, consider the following ground rules:

- When someone raises a question or comment that is off the main topic, suggest you deal with it another time, or, if you feel led to go in that direction, let the group know that you will be spending some time discussing it.
- If someone asks a question that you don't know how to answer, admit it, and move on. At your discretion, feel free to invite group members to comment on questions that call for personal experience.
- If you find that one or two people are dominating the discussion time, direct a few questions to others in the group. Outside the main group time, ask the more dominating members to help you draw out the quieter ones. Work to make them part of the solution instead of part of the problem.
- When a disagreement occurs, encourage the group members to process the matter in love. Encourage those on opposite sides to restate what they heard the other side say about the matter, and then invite each side to evaluate if that perception is accurate. Lead the group in examining other scriptures related to the topic and look for common ground.

When any of these issues arise, encourage your group members to follow these words from Scripture: "Love one another" (John 13:34); "If possible, as far as it depends on you, live at peace with everyone" (Romans 12:18); "Whatever is true . . . noble . . . right . . . pure . . . lovely . . . if anything is excellent or praiseworthy—think about such things" (Philippians 4:8); and "Everyone should be quick to listen, slow to speak and slow to become angry" (James 1:19). This will make your group time more rewarding and beneficial for everyone who attends.

Thank you again for taking the time to lead your group. You are making a difference in your group members' lives and having an impact on their journey toward understanding the gift of wine as they learn to engage with God using all their senses, including touch, taste, and smell.

NOTES

1. Gisela H. Kreglinger, *Cup Overflowing: Wine's Place in Faith, Feasting, and Fellowship* (Grand Rapids: Zondervan Reflective 2024), 6.
2. Gisela H. Kreglinger, *The Spirituality of Wine* (Grand Rapids, MI: Eerdmans, 2016), 31.
3. Gisela H. Kreglinger, *The Soul of Wine: Savoring the Goodness of God* (Downers Grove, IL: InterVarsity Press, 2019), 148.
4. Saint John Chrysostom, cited in Kreglinger, *The Spirituality of Wine*, 42.
5. Gisela H. Kreglinger, *Cup Overflowing*, 6.
6. Kreglinger, *Cup Overflowing*, 136.
7. See Kreglinger, *The Soul of Wine*, 6.
8. Kreglinger, *The Soul of Wine*, 18.
9. Kreglinger, *The Soul of Wine*, 4.
10. Kreglinger, *Cup Overflowing*, 9.
11. Kreglinger, *Cup Overflowing*, 16.
12. Kreglinger, *Cup Overflowing*, 14.
13. Kreglinger, *The Spirituality of Wine*, 34.
14. Kreglinger, *Cup Overflowing, 208. See also Lothar Becker, Rebe, Rausch und Religion: Eine kulturgeschichtliche Studie zum Wein in der Bibel* (Muenster, Germany: LIT, 1999), 194.
15. Kreglinger, *The Spirituality of Wine*, 220.
16. Kreglinger, *The Spirituality of Wine*, 65.
17. Kreglinger, *Cup Overflowing*, 117.
18. Kreglinger, *Cup Overflowing*, 56.
19. Kreglinger, *The Spirituality of Wine*, 65.
20. Kreglinger, *The Spirituality of Wine*, 215.
21. Kreglinger, *Cup Overflowing*, 4.
22. Kreglinger, *Cup Overflowing*, 188.
23. Kreglinger, *The Soul of Wine*, 3.
24. Rozanne Frazee and Randy Frazee, *Real Simplicity: Making Room for Life* (Grand Rapids: Zondervan, 2011), 90.
25. Kreglinger, *Cup Overflowing*, 50.
26. You can find an enlightening discussion of the theological depth of this film in *The Spirituality of Wine.* Many of the details of the feast contain references to biblical themes.
27. To help you understand the many biblical references and rich theology of food and feasting in this film, see Kreglinger, *The Spirituality of Wine, 88ff.*
28. Martin Luther, "The Fourth Sermon, March 12, 1522, Wednesday after Invocavit," *Weimarer Ausgabe* (WA), 10/III, translated by Gisela H. Kreglinger.
29. Kreglinger, *Cup Overflowing*, 2.
30. Kreglinger, *Cup Overflowing*, 172-173.
31. Kreglinger, *Cup Overflowing*, 164-165.
32. Kate Julian, "America Has a Drinking Problem," *The Atlantic,* July/August 2021, www.theatlantic.com/magazine/archive/2021/07/america-drinking-alone-problem/619017/.
33. Kreglinger, *Cup Overflowing*, 161.
34. Kreglinger, *Cup Overflowing*, 38.
35. Kreglinger, *The Soul of Wine,* 94–95.
36. Gerard Manly Hopkins, "God's Grandeur," 1877.
37. William Wordsworth, "The World Is Too Much with Us," published in *Poems, in Two Volumes* (1807).
38. If you have any feelings of intimidation around wine, read the "From Intimidation to Appreciation" chapter in *The Soul of Wine* by Gisela H. Kreglinger
39. Kreglinger, *Cup Overflowing*, 120.
40. Simone Weil, *Waiting for God* (New York: Harper Perennial, 2009), 99–105.